"Away With Stereotyped Mormons!"

❧❦❧

"Away With Stereotyped Mormons!"

Thoughts on Individuality, Perfection, and the Broad Expanse of Eternity

❧❦❧

Roger Terry

Rendsburg Publishing

Rendsburg Publishing
1908 N. 400 E.
Orem, UT 84057
Tel: 801-221-1271   Fax: 801-221-1271

Ordering Information
Individual Sales. Individual copies of this book can be ordered direct from Rendsburg Publishing at the address above.

Quantity Sales. Special discounts are available on quantity purchases. For details, contact Rendsburg Publishing at the address above.

Orders by U.S. trade bookstores and wholesalers. Please contact Origin Book Sales, 6200 South 380 West, Murray, Utah 84107; tel. 801-268-9890; 888-467-4446; fax 801-268-9895.

Printed in the United States of America

Library of Congress Catalog Card Number: 96-67607
Terry, Roger, 1956–
     "Away with stereotyped Mormons!" : thoughts on individuality,
perfection, and the broad expanse of eternity / Roger Terry.
          p.   cm.
     Includes bibliographical references and index.
     ISBN 0–9651483–0–0
     1. Theology—Church of Jesus Christ of Latter-day Saints.   2. Church of
Jesus Christ of Latter-day Saints.   3. Mormons.
I. Title.

First Edition
     99 98 97 96   10 9   8   7   6   5   4   3   2   1

*To those who know they are
but strangers and pilgrims
on this telestial sphere.
May they find what they seek:
their destiny and their eternal home.*

Contents

Introduction

Beyond Primary

"Who are you?" the German boy asked as we approached the apartment building where he lived. He was perhaps five years old, was playing out on the sidewalk, and had apparently never encountered two young men dressed in suits and ties before. Missionaries were a new item to be curious about in his expanding world. "Who are you?"

"We're Japanese," I teased flippantly, knowing he had no idea where Japan was, if he had even heard of it at all.

His brow furrowed, and he squinted at me in the failing light of evening. Then, in that innate way children have of distinguishing between important and unimportant things, he turned away and began playing again. We left him there, entered the apartment building, and started ringing doorbells, hoping in vain that a searching soul or two would let us in to tell them about who they really were.

In the context of an entire mission and against the backdrop of a handful of truly significant experiences, this little scenario should have quickly faded from memory. But for some reason I can't forget that little boy—perhaps because I can't forget his question.

"Who are you?" children ask. A simple, direct question. And they aim it as readily at adults as at the new kid on the block. "Who are you?" A child's question. A question we adults do not ask of each other. An uncomfortable question. Perhaps we feel we would be prying, trespassing. So we ask more superficial, telling questions: "What's your name?" "Where do you work?" "Where are you from?" And what we are really saying is: "Define yourself in terms of how you make a living, or what your parents chose to call you, or who you married, or where you happen to live." We don't ask each other such personal, penetrating questions as "Who are you?" Perhaps we avoid this question because we suspect that the other person does not—just as we do not—know quite how to answer.

So, who are you? Separate from occupation, address, income tax bracket, ethnic heritage, marital status, home town, assumed public image, even name—who are you? How would you answer? Who am I? I am not Japanese, and even if I had answered the little German boy's question with "missionaries" or "Mormons" or "Americans," I'm not sure any of these semitruthful answers would have been any more satisfactory than the one I flippantly tossed his way. In our hectic, cluttered, adult lives, do we ever find time—perhaps just before we drift off into well-earned sleep or maybe while we're brushing our teeth in front of the mirror— to ponder our own identity?

Who am I? Am I just a bundle of habits and attitudes—a male biological unit who mows the lawn every Saturday, eats more junk food than is healthy, drives too fast, watches too much TV, tries in vain to persuade his kids to stop quarreling, struggles to make ends meet, and singlehandedly turns the monthly budget into another exercise in futility? Is that who I am? Isn't there some deeper, more fundamental level of identity?

Any primary child could answer that question without even thinking. "I am a child of God." Of course. We've all sung it countless times, accepting with unthinking and humble pride that this is one of the luminous, eternal truths that distinguish us from other religions, never pondering the significant questions behind the Primary child's answer. Yes, I am a child of God; but so is everyone else. Am I then just a clone of some eternal pattern? Or am I unique? Am I, in an eternal sense, different from everyone else, with my own individual personality and eternal potential?

"But wait," someone will say. "We're not supposed to busy ourselves with such imponderables. 'I am a child of God' is as far as we're supposed to go. The gospel is supposed to be simply beautiful and beautifully simple. Why should we waste time with questions that have perplexed gentile philosophers for millennia, when we have THE TRUTH? I mean, it's all so simple. If we keep the commandments, learn 'what we must do,' we'll return 'to live with him some day.'"

Yes, it's all so simple and beautiful. Just keep the commandments, and don't bother trying to figure out past and future—who we were in the pre-existence and what our eternal potential is. The present is all we need to worry about. And anyway, the present is much too hectic to allow ourselves to be distracted by perturbing philosophical quandaries. We're too busy to worry about unanswered eternal questions. If we're supposed to know anything about these issues, the prophet will tell us. Or will he? When I read what the Prophet Joseph once said, I sense in his words a deep yearning after an eternal perspective, a hunger for infinite knowledge, and a certainty that everyday worldly concerns—and not eternal mysteries—are the real distractions.

"I have tried for a number of years," said Joseph, "to get the minds of the Saints prepared to receive the things of God," but they "fly to pieces like glass as soon as anything comes that is contrary to their traditions: they still cannot stand the fire at all."[1] "How vain and trifling have been our spirits, our conferences, our councils, our meetings, our private as well as public conversations," Joseph wrote also, "—too low, too mean, too vulgar, too condescending for the dignified characters of the called and chosen of God."[2]

Brigham Young was equally critical of the saints' unwillingness to interchange ideas and detect and correct their errors. Such hesitancy produces "too much of a sameness in this community."[3] "I am not a stereotyped Latter-day Saint," Brother Brigham proclaimed, "and do not believe in the doctrine. . . . Are we going to stand still? Away with stereotyped 'Mormons'!"[4] The sameness Brigham Young decried is caused by mental lethargy, an unwillingness to raise our thinking and our conversations to appropriate adult levels—to ask adult questions and seek adult answers.

Primary answers are fine for Primary children, but we mustn't get locked into a Primary mentality. If we do indeed learn "all that we must do," so that we will "live with him some day," then we might well ask the question: How will we live with him? As children? Certainly not. We are children of God, but he doesn't expect us to remain that way. And anyway, what does it really mean to be a child of God? Our children in mortality are not really ours. We do not possess them. And in spite of some genetic baggage they inherit, they are nonetheless independent, individually accountable beings. What then is our real relationship to our heavenly parents?

We know so little about eternity, our natural environment. This earth life is, in more ways than one, very much like my mission years ago in Germany. When I arrived I didn't speak the language. I knew I was supposed to accomplish several purposes before I came home, and discovering those purposes was a long process. I had both significant and insignificant experiences that changed me in definite ways, and after a time I honestly couldn't remember what it was like to be "home." Germany became home to me. So what is our natural element? What is our eternal home like? Who are we really? Is it so wasteful to wonder about these things?

"Let the solemnities of eternity rest upon your minds" (D&C 43:34), the Lord says. Is it wrong to seek glimpses of the infinite? Is it wrong to ponder difficult questions, to try to fit our mortal experiences into an eternal context? How do we know what God will or will not reveal until we press him for knowledge? His promises suggest we underestimate his willingness.

The chapters of this book explore some unspoken ramifications of truths we sometimes take for granted. We'll reason about eternity and about our general identity as children of God. We'll talk about individuality and its implications. We'll confront the perplexing dilemma of self—of balancing the search for identity with both today's trendy addiction to self-esteem and the "outmoded" notion of selflessness. And we will briefly discuss some attitudes we should cultivate if we want to achieve our individual potential as children of God. I hope you enjoy these thoughts. My sole intention is to share something of value with you, in hope that it may cause you to think more deeply about who you are, who you can become, how you relate to others—and why this earth life is so vitally, pivotally important.

1

The Question of Intelligence

Our search for an eternal identity must begin, according to mortal logic, at the beginning. There is, however, one small flaw in this approach—there was no beginning. Intelligence, the part of us that thinks and gives us existence, "was not created or made, neither indeed can be" (D&C 93:29). "The mind or the intelligence which man possesses is co-equal [co-eternal] with God himself. . . . Intelligence is eternal and exists upon a self-existent principle."[1]

In his excellent book on the pre-existence, *The Life Before*, Brent L. Top explains that the Church has never taken an official stand on one very fundamental question: Have we or have we not always existed as individual intelligent beings? Unfortunately, the Prophet's statements leave the issue somewhat cloudy. One school of thought asserts that we did not exist as individual, conscious beings prior to our spirit birth, at which time our heavenly parents organized our spirits from impersonal eternal elements known as "intelligence." The counterargument states that each person (personality) has always existed, first as a bodiless entity called "an intelligence," then as an intelligence clothed with a spirit body, and now as a spirit endowed with a mortal, physical body. Brother Top explains both positions, remaining appropriately uncommitted to either side (since he is writing as a member of the BYU religion faculty). Because I am writing without such contraints, however, I will venture to express an opinion on the matter and support it with reasonable arguments. In fact, I'm going to choose sides—with the likes of B.H. Roberts and Orson Pratt—and explain the inescapable illogic I see in the first school of thought.

Inequality

The first inconsistency in the idea that we were organized from some eternal but impersonal material called intelligence is the inequality of spirits. Spirits, in the pre-existence, were infinitely varied. Most, if not all, had flaws and weaknesses—in varying degrees. All had talents and strengths—in different areas. We know that some talents were more refined than others in our pre-earthly existence. This hints of an innate predisposition in spirits toward the development of certain qualities. And this predisposition suggests an unequal start, an unequal original makeup. I am certain, for instance, that Mozart began his "spirit childhood" in the pre-existence with a much greater talent or ability in music than I had. Einstein undoubtedly had greater theoretical capacity than most of us. Each of us began at different levels in different areas of talent and intelligence. We certainly were not identical, not made from the same pattern, as it were.

This logic also holds true on the other side of the ledger. Each of us, excepting Jesus, has brought to earth various weaknesses that were certainly not first developed in the glorious premortal home of our heavenly parents. In essence, I don't believe that I started out perfect and then gradually developed the tendency to criticize, to be impatient, or to lose my temper. Logic insists that the basic flaw, the predisposition, was present when I became a spirit child of God, since those of us who graduated to the second estate progressed rather than regressed as spirit children.

At any rate, it is apparent that spirits did not start on an equal footing, except that we were all made innocent at our spirit birth. But just as at baptism, being made pure does not necessarily remove flaws and weaknesses. Some in the pre-existence had greater strengths in certain areas; some had greater weaknesses. One, in particular, was far ahead of the rest of us. Jehovah, the Firstborn, was so like our Heavenly Father that he became a member of the Godhead before he ever received a mortal body. The most reasonable explanation of this fact is that our Heavenly Father chose, for obvious reasons, the most noble and advanced of all the intelligences, to become his Firstborn.

The only other possible explanation seems cruel and incomprehensible. If intelligence is merely some kind of impersonal spiritual building material, then why would God take the best of it and create one perfect Son, then use the left-overs to produce billions upon billions of inferior, flawed, and problematic younger siblings?

This explanation is entirely unsatisfactory. Christ's superiority cannot be explained in terms of a preferential God, or a God who made one flawless creation, only to lose the blueprint. How could a perfect God—using an unaware, impersonal, unself-conscious spirit element—create countless highly imperfect, self-aware beings? Simply put, Christ's unrivaled brilliance and our various levels of comparative dimness had to be eternal, and it was in everyone's best interest that Christ was chosen first to take his proper place as the incomparable Firstborn of the Father.

Spirit Birth

Scripture tells us that God is the father of spirits and that Christ is the Firstborn. I do not believe this reference to parenthood and birth is in any way metaphorical. Revealed truth insists that we can become like God and have an eternal increase—that husband and wife, sealed by the priesthood in celestial marriage, will have spirit offspring throughout eternity (see D&C 132.) If this is indeed true, and exalted man and woman can unite to generate spirit offspring in a manner similar to the process of mortal conception and birth, then we must ask one question. How could it be possible for the union of two exalted, perfected beings to bring forth imperfect, widely diverse offspring?

The only reasonable answer lies in the idea that they are merely providing spirit bodies for already existing and imperfect intelligences. Otherwise, we must assume that all the best genetic material was spent on the Firstborn, and that our heavenly parents could never again duplicate the standard set by their first child, Jehovah.

Such an idea is unreasonable. It makes much more sense to assume that our spirit birth was very like our mortal birth. The acquisition of a spirit body merely enhanced the potential of our intelligences, just as the gift of a physical body enhances the possibilities of our spirits. And, of course, just as we inherit certain traits from our earthly parents, we can assume that we inherited noble and godly traits from our heavenly parents. But this noble inheritance merely adds to, and does not create, the being who receives it.

Satan

As problematic as Jehovah's superiority is in trying to support the intelligence-as-impersonal-raw-material argument, Lucifer's very existence is even more inexplicable. God sees the end from the beginning. He knew, when he organized the spirit son named Lucifer, that he was creating a vessel doomed to suffer the horrible torments of eternal hell. Would a compassionate God create from oblivion a conscious being, a son whom he would love, if he knew with a perfect knowledge that that son would spend eternity in hellish torment? Not if intelligence was merely a mass of raw, impersonal material, to be used as God saw fit. Such an act would be nothing less than sadism. God would create a spirit son like Lucifer only if the essence of that spirit, its personality and uniqueness, already existed and deserved (notwithstanding God's foreknowledge of the ultimate outcome) the chance to progress or at least earn his destiny.

Likewise, God knows our ultimate destination—and many of us, because of disobedience, will not return to live with him—but that does not stop him from giving us every opportunity to earn our reward or punishment. Each of us has an eternal destiny that lies beyond God's power to determine. We are responsible for our ultimate salvation or damnation. He merely assists us, without interfering in our free agency.

Granted, there is a need for Satan, for the opposition he supplies. Without Satan we would be handicapped in our attempt to become like God. But I don't for one instant believe that God would create out of the impersonal elements of oblivion a conscious being doomed to eternal torment simply so that others of his weak and imperfect creations could experience opposition and adversity.

Accountability

If we assume that God organized spirits from some kind of collective spiritual element called intelligence, and that before this creative act those spirits did not exist as conscious, individual beings, then God did in fact create something—a conscious, self-aware, independent personality—where before there was nothing. And if this is the case, the creation of the spirit signifies the inception of agency.

We know that spirits had agency in the pre-existence. But I argue that if God created a conscious entity from unconscious elements, knowing perfectly at the outset that this particular new being contained flaws and weaknesses and had no chance whatever (in God's mind, at least, since he sees the end from the beginning) to become exalted, then God would be accountable for that being's damnation. Why? Because he created it with insurmountable weaknesses, which it had no choice in acquiring. That may sound like heresy, but if God, using impersonal "intelligence" as his potter's clay, chooses for some reason to make one spirit adequately strong and another hopelessly flawed, then the ultimate exaltation or damnation of the individual is largely his doing.

Now, we do not believe in a deterministic God. We believe in a God who has perfect foreknowledge. But the God described by this particular school of thought does indeed play a deterministic role in the lives of his children—by the choice of elements he employs in their creation—therefore, the ultimate accountability would be his.

We may argue that no weakness is insurmountable, that we can choose to accept God's grace and overcome our weaknesses, so that "weak things become strong" unto us (Ether 12:27). Our ultimate destiny is then a product of our choices, regardless of any disadvantage we may have been given at the outset. But if we were burdened before we were ever capable of choice with fundamental weaknesses—such as a basic incapacity to even plant the seed of faith—how can we be accountable for not having the faith to accept God's grace and overcome that weakness? It's a Catch-22. Our strengths and weaknesses always influence our choices. Sometimes we are simply too weak to choose correctly. Sometimes we are too weak to even ask for strength. If God creates us, knowing from the outset that we will not choose to become as he is—and this is a very real scenario for the majority—why would he create us that way? Why wouldn't he create us differently, make us more like Christ?

The notion of sin also argues against this theory. Sin is more than simple bad behavior. Sin results from weakness. If we had no weakness, we would not sin. Christ was sinless because he was not weak. He was tempted in all points, undoubtedly more severely than any of God's other children, yet he never succumbed. Someone once said: "Sin is not ignorance; it is insanity." This is true. When we have no knowledge of appropriate behavior and attitudes, we are not accountable. Sin occurs when we know the law, but act against our better judgment. Sometimes we act against better judgment out of rebellion, but usually this is not the case. Most often we are simply too weak to withstand temptation, too weak to invoke God's saving grace. So, if our weaknesses are God's doing, because he used an inferior quality of "intelligence" when he put us together, then we cannot be accountable for our failure to measure up. "It's not my fault," any of us could argue, "that God didn't use top-quality intelligence when he organized my spirit. It's not my fault that he didn't make me more like the Savior."

The only logical explanation for the fact that we are *completely* accountable for our actions is that we have always existed, that our weaknesses and strengths are an intrinsic part of us, and that we have always been accountable for them. This makes perfect sense. If I am given a spirit body and the opportunity to both expand my innate strengths and overcome my inherent weaknesses, it is I who am wholly accountable for my success or failure, and my agency is totally unimpaired. In this theory, instead of being a preferential determiner of destinies, an omnipotent playwright who dreams up an infinitely varied cast to perform his eternal play, God becomes a compassionate volunteer, aiding in our eternal progress, but never infringing on our eternal agency to become whatever we choose. The only logical explanation for our free agency and complete accountability is the eternal existence of identity.

Our Relationship to God

At this point, we should probably take a step backward and say to ourselves: "That's all fine and good and interesting, but is it important? Isn't it a tangent, sheer intellectual speculation? Do I really need to think about it? It doesn't affect my salvation." Perhaps, perhaps not. Personally, I think the question discussed here is more than just interesting. Granted, we can be saved without a sure knowledge on the subject, but Joseph Smith felt it of sufficient import that he spoke of it at length.

This whole question of "intelligence versus intelligences" is more than a frivolous quest to discover our origins—to find out who we really are. It is also a quest to discover the true nature of God and our relationship to him. If he created our consciousness, we have a much different relationship to him than if he merely provided spirit bodies for our already extant minds and identities.

God said to Abraham: "I rule . . . over all the intelligences thine eyes have seen from the beginning; I came down in the beginning in the midst of all the intelligences thou hast seen" (Abraham 3:21). The beginning here apparently refers to the beginning of our relationship with the Father. He came down in the midst of all the intelligences. We can infer from this statement that at some point he came to us, when we were intelligences, and that point marked a "beginning."

Joseph Smith explains this further: "God himself, finding he was in the midst of spirits and glory, because he was more intelligent, saw proper to institute laws whereby the rest could have a privilege to advance like himself. The relationship we have with God places us in a situation to advance in knowledge. He has power to institute laws to instruct the weaker intelligences, that they may be exalted with himself."[2] Our relationship with God is indeed one of dependence, for without him we could not progress to become like him. But we are not creations of his, composed like music, at his whim and for his pleasure. We are more like a simple melody that God found, already intact, and transformed into a complex symphonic score. How well we perform the symphony determines our ultimate destiny. We existed before the "beginning" in a rudimentary, undeveloped state. But God came to us and, seeing that we were deserving of the chance to advance to higher levels of existence, gave us spirit bodies and an eternal plan and instituted laws by which we could grow and progress.

The Mind

When Joseph says God found himself in the midst of spirits, the context of the King Follett discourse, from which this quote is taken, indicates that by "spirits" he means "intelligences" rather than beings endowed with spirit bodies born of exalted parents. In the paragraphs preceding this statement we read: "God never had the power to create the spirit of man at all. . . . Intelligence is eternal and exists upon a self-existent principle. It is a spirit from age to age, and there is no creation about it. All the minds and spirits that God ever sent into the world are susceptible of enlargement."[3]

We know that our heavenly parents created our spirit bodies. When Joseph says God doesn't have the power to create our spirits, he is obviously referring to our minds, our intelligences. B. H. Roberts, in a footnote to this statement, also points out that Joseph refers to intelligence as a spirit, not just spirit, "that is, an entity, a person, an individual." From Joseph's words quoted above (and others in the King Follett discourse), we recognize a distinction between the mind and the spirit body. The mind of man, which God cannot create, is as distinct from the spirit body as the spirit is from the physical body. The mind is the key to our identity. It is not the spirit that thinks, that reasons, that holds concepts and prejudices and opinions and serves as the reservoir for personality. It is the mind, the intelligence. The mind is, of course, influenced and shaped by the experiences of both the spirit body and the physical body, but it is nonetheless distinct.

What the mind or intelligence is, exactly, we do not know. It is apparently a spirit of sorts, perhaps an unformed spirit essence. It is obviously not in human form, as are the spirit bodies our heavenly parents created for us—otherwise, creating those spirit bodies would have been a redundant act. The intelligence, therefore, must be a unique, eternal, uncreated, self-motivated, fully aware entity—in other words, an individual.

2

The Opposite Sex

If we are to explore the question of eternal identity, we cannot sidestep the particularly controversial question of gender. It is a fact that some of us are female and some of us are male, and in recent years this incontrovertible and simple notion has been burdened with unpleasant though not groundless accusations, resentful indignation, and numerous attempts to discount its most basic implications. Some in the Church have decried the perceived second-class status of women; some, not understanding the meaning of the word, have crusaded for equality; and a few, apparently assuming that lobbying is an appropriate and effective means of changing God's mind, have even called for the priesthood to be extended to the sisters.

It is not my purpose here to discuss this particular can of worms. Personally, I don't know why men are allowed to hold the priesthood and women are not. Nor do I pretend to understand either the ins and outs of governing the universe or how the inherent responsibilities are divvied up. I do, however, have a few ideas that may help us understand gender in terms of our eternal identity.

Opposition

Consider what President Joseph Fielding Smith once said: "Some of the functions in the celestial body will not appear in the terrestrial body, neither in the telestial body, and the power of procreation will be removed. I take it that men and women will, in these kingdoms, be just what the so-called Christian world expects us all to be—neither man nor woman, merely immortal beings having received the resurrection."[1] That is an incredible idea, if we understand what he's saying. The physical distinction between male and female will only exist in the celestial kingdom. Why? The reason, I believe, has something to do with opposition.

One of the most maligned of all scriptural passages is Lehi's treatise on opposition. "For it must needs be, that there is an opposition in all things" (2 Nephi 2:11). Every sacrament meeting talk I have ever heard on the topic of adversity has used this statement to explain the notion that life has to be hard, that we all have to experience trials and tribulations, that in order to grow we must be opposed. Now, I'm not arguing the truth of these assertions, but I have often wondered why we use Lehi's words to substantiate this claim, for that is not at all what he was talking about.

As a side note, I think we often underestimate Father Lehi. It's easy to think of him as an old man, an inadequate parent who couldn't quite figure out how to handle Laman and Lemuel. The story of how Nephi more or less took charge and built a boat and led the family across the ocean to the promised land may give us reason to assume that Lehi was just an old, failing man. It's not difficult to sort of shove him into the background. But before we do, we'd best remember that he confounded Laman and Lemuel with his words and with the Spirit. Beyond that, he understood his vision of the tree of life intuitively, a vision that the angel had to explain to Nephi in detail. Also, his words to his son Jacob in the second chapter of 2 Nephi reveal a vital, active, probing mind, even when his body was ready to return to the dust. His message to Jacob is one of the most brilliant in all of holy writ.

> For it must needs be, that there is an opposition in all things. If not so, . . . righteousness could not be brought to pass, neither wickedness, neither holiness nor misery, neither good nor bad. Wherefore, all things must needs be a compound in one; wherefore, if it should be one body it must needs remain as dead, having no life neither death, nor corruption nor incorruption, happiness nor misery, neither sense nor insensibility.
>
> Wherefore, it must needs have been created for a thing of naught; wherefore there would have been no purpose in the end of its creation. Wherefore, this thing must needs destroy the wisdom of God and his eternal purposes, and also the power, and the mercy, and the justice of God. (2 Nephi 2:11-12)

The opposition Lehi is talking about is not the opposition of adversity; it is the opposition of oppositeness. And the notion of oppositeness delves directly into the heart of existence itself. If there is no opposition, there is no existence. If there is no good, there can be no bad. If there is no right, there can be no left. If there is no light, there can be no darkness. "But wait," some may say. "If there is no light, then everything would be darkness." Perhaps, but the word darkness would be absolutely meaningless. Our existence is defined by opposites. Without opposites nothing would have meaning. Health would go completely unappreciated if we had no knowledge of sickness and pain. Indeed, the idea of health would be unfathomable. If everything were darkness, light would be an incomprehensible, useless idea, as it is for the blind. We define a thing in the context of its opposite. If the opposite ceases to exist, the thing in question becomes meaningless—a thing of naught. And if there were no opposites at all, everything would be a "compound in one" and there would be no existence.

The implications of this doctrine in terms of gender are fairly obvious. If there is no male, then being female is meaningless (as it is, for instance, to lesbians). If there is no female, then the idea of being male is mere emptiness. The two conditions define each other. We know what being female means because we can compare it with its opposite. And we know what being male means because of its opposite. Of course, we men don't understand completely what it means to be female, because we don't really know what being female is like. And the reverse is also true. But we do know much from observation and communication. We recognize differences, and those differences, as science is now demonstrating, go far beyond the physical. In fact, I suggest that if there were not fundamental nonphysical differences between men and women, there would be little reason for the physical differences.

To put it simply, men and women are eternally dissimilar in nature. And only the complete understanding of each opposing role will result in fulfillment of the eternal purpose, destiny, and identity of the human species. Only in the highest level of the celestial kingdom, where one cannot dwell singly, is our ultimate, eternal purpose fulfilled. A large portion of that purpose is to enable other intelligences to follow the same celestial path we are now following, a purpose that cannot be fulfilled by single, unisex gods. Certainly another part of that purpose is to enjoy perfect happiness in the glory of an eternally oppositional (though not adversarial) marriage relationship. Apparently our joy can only be full in that marvelous marriage of opposites.

By the same token, joy is comparatively dimmed in the terrestrial and telestial kingdoms, where such relationships do not exist. We call life in these kingdoms damnation. A thing that is damned cannot reach its ultimate destination. I was fascinated by the account of Dr. George Ritchie in *Return from Tomorrow*, who, while clinically dead, experienced a sort of out-of-body tour by a being of light, who he understood was the Savior. The conditions he describes conform uncannily with our unique LDS understanding of the three degrees of glory.

He beheld only at a great distance what we would call the celestial glory, a glory Joseph Smith was permitted to see up close and in detail. But it was his account of the middle condition that fascinated me. He saw a peaceful world that reminded him of a well-planned university. "Except," he says, "that to compare what I was now seeing with anything on earth was ridiculous. It was more as if all the schools and colleges in the world were only piecemeal reproductions of this reality." His description of the inhabitants of this realm is of interest:

> I could not tell if they were men or women, old or young, for all were covered from head to foot in loose-flowing hooded cloaks which made me think vaguely of monks. But the atmosphere of the place was not at all as I imagined a monastery. It was more like some tremendous study center, humming with the excitement of great discovery. Everyone we passed in the wide halls and on the curving staircases seemed caught up in some all-engrossing activity; not many words were exchanged among them. And yet I sensed no unfriendliness between these beings, rather an aloofness of total concentration.[2]

It is interesting that he couldn't tell whether the inhabitants of this realm were male or female, for they all dressed alike. No clothing or grooming to either distinguish the sexes or make them attractive to each other. That was simply no longer a part of their make-up. The people he saw spent all their time in the pursuit of knowledge. He heard music—of a complexity he couldn't fathom—being composed and performed. He walked through an enormous library that he understood contained the great books of the universe, including one room that contained the "central thought of this earth." (Imagine, the notion of a universe filled with peopled worlds was not mere conjecture—it was a foregone conclusion.)

The people in this realm were totally self-absorbed in the quest for knowledge. And this makes sense. In the absence of a higher, eternal purpose, what would be left for purified, immortal, unexalted beings? Inhabitants of the telestial and terrestrial glories choose by their actions to deny their eternal identities and, hence, cannot fulfill the end of their creation. They cannot fulfill their eternal purpose, and thus become things of naught—neither male nor female—beings with no eternal lives, no eternally expanding future.

If there is anything we should learn from this picture of the terrestrial and telestial kingdoms, it is that we should be careful about minimizing the differences—including differences in roles and responsibilities—between men and women. We should realize that those who seek to create a world where men and women serve society in identical ways are imagining the terrestrial glory as their ideal for a perfect heaven. In reality, the highest glory will go to those who recognize and maximize the inherent oppositeness of the sexes.

Our ultimate destiny, if we are true to our eternal identity, is the celestial glory, where both femaleness and maleness will reach their full potential. We must assume that this oppositeness is not merely a mortal acquisition, but an eternal distinction. Spirits in the pre-existence were not ungendered. That we know. We must therefore assume that intelligences also, in some way, exhibited among themselves this type of opposition. And the opposition at this most fundamental level is likely the very heart of the nonphysical differences between men and women.

What then are the consequences of denying or eradicating these differences? One consequence is losing them permanently. Those who either ignore or abuse or tempt God to erase the differences between men and women risk having him do just that.

School

Mortality has been likened to a school, an educational experience in which we are graded on both desire and performance, and rewarded accordingly. What I have suggested in this chapter is that men and women are in the same school, mortality, but each gender has been given its own customized curriculum. Some things that men are asked to do may not be beneficial in the eternal sense for women, and vice versa. Our task, it seems, is to discover who we are, and then take those courses that enhance our eternal identity. Part of the curriculum, of course, is general education, and both women and men—if they wish to graduate— must enroll. By the same token, some classes are taught only to individual students, regardless of gender. A great danger arises, however, if our identity and potential require us to be in one major and yet we, for some reason, insist on another.

A personal experience may illustrate. When I returned from my mission and enrolled at Brigham Young University, I had no idea what I should pursue as a career. I finally decided on accounting as a major, figuring that I could make a good living at it. But the further I progressed toward my degree, the more intensely I felt that I was on the wrong path. I felt that something fundamental, something deep inside, was being assaulted, twisted, changed. What I was studying was diametrically opposed to what I was supposed to become. Something vital was dying inside. Sensitivity and feeling were vanishing. I felt I was being turned into a cold, calculating machine. Finally, when I couldn't stand it any longer, I changed majors to German, which had previously been my minor. The sense of peace, of rightness and perfect fit, that followed the decision was notable. I somehow came to know that if I spent my life as an accountant, a significant portion of my unique identity would be stunted, shifted into a dead-end path. But the important lesson from this experience was this: Sometimes it is through discovering who we aren't that we discover who we really are. Opposition. This experience helped me understand some basic parts of my identity that until then had been unfocused from of a lack of contrast.

So it is also in the school of mortality. We sometimes seek admittance into the wrong major. Some of us, in terms of gender questions and roles and responsibilities, are zealously pursuing a curriculum that will either lead our identities into dead ends or render us unable to graduate. If, for instance, I am an engineering major and instead of taking engineering courses spend my time studying linguistics and art and history, and then expect to be granted a degree in engineering—well, to put it mildly, I'm not handling the realities of university life very well. I may have learned many interesting, even useful, ideas, but if I'm supposed to become an engineer, I must follow the designed curriculum.

Likewise, if I am a man, and my eternal destiny is to become an exalted man, I must follow the curriculum that will enable me to reach that potential. Although I do not understand completely why this is so (and although there are always some exceptions), priesthood, fatherhood, and providing for a family are typical courses in this curriculum. Conversely, a course called Mr. Mom 101 is not recognized by the major department.

The fact is, there are eternal differences between men and women. They are meant to complement and not to mimic each other. And in our search for identity, we must not discount this fundamental principle of opposition.

3

Time and Thought

Both logic and revelation insist that it is important for us to have a correct understanding of God. The Prophet Joseph taught: "Let us here observe, that three things are necessary in order that any rational and intelligent being may exercise faith in God unto life and salvation. First, the idea that he actually exists. Secondly, a correct idea of his character, perfections, and attributes. Thirdly, an actual knowledge that the course of life which he is pursuing is according to his will."[1] A correct understanding of God's character, perfections, and attributes is not only a prerequisite for faith in God, but also helps us understand our own potential, our eternal destiny.

Sometimes, though, our finite minds tend to project our current circumstances and experiences into the eternal realms. We find ourselves assuming that life there will more or less reflect our experiences here, except that that world will be filled with peace and joy, whereas this one includes pain and sin and conflict. Some specific things we know about the Father and other celestial beings, however, suggest that the fundamental way they experience reality is much different from the way we mortals perceive our earthly surroundings.

Intelligence

We read that "the glory of God is intelligence" (D&C 93:36). But what is intelligence? Reading further in the same verse, we find the answer: intelligence is "light and truth." Good, but what is light? Joseph Smith described the Father and Son as radiating a brightness that exceeded that of the sun. I don't for one second believe that Joseph was being metaphorical. And even my severely impaired understanding of physics suggests some incredible possibilities. Let me hazard this much speculation: Our eyes are limited to seeing a rather narrow segment of the electromagnetic spectrum that we call the visible spectrum. We see from violet to red, but we can't see ultraviolet or infrared waves. And yet there is a whole spectrum of rays, from the shortest gamma rays to the longest radio waves—and most of it is invisible to our eyes. Our brains also emit waves that can be detected with sensitive instruments, though mortal eyes cannot see them. But what if celestial eyes can see beyond our visible spectrum.

We have accounts by a few individuals who have been quickened and thereby permitted to see beyond the veil, and they report colors that are not part of our mortal experience. What if God's intelligence is actually light, not in a metaphorical sense, but light of a different frequency, perhaps, and too intense for our mortal eyes to either behold or endure? I've heard it said that the veil between us and the immortal realms is our physical body. Perhaps our mortal eyes prevent us from seeing the full light of

God. Perhaps this is for our own protection—until we are ready. Suffice it to say that in a very real way, which we do not understand, God is light. He radiates light, and that light has something to do with his intelligence.

But what is truth? In section 93, verse 24, we read: "Truth is knowledge of things as they are, and as they were, and as they are to come." Knowledge of past, present, and future. So, we reason, God is one up on us. We know only the present and the past; he knows the future, too. But such thinking is rather self-congratulatory and presumptuous. I think I can make a good argument for the fact that God is more than "one up on us," that, indeed, we know neither past, present, nor future.

We don't know the past. Yes, we have memory, but memory is quite different from *knowing* the past. Memory is limited by two facts. First, it is incredibly unreliable. It is like a series of faded snapshots. I have a fairly good memory, I believe. (My wife would argue that it's also selective.) For instance, I can still remember the phone numbers of several boys I played little league baseball with, numbers I haven't called in years. When I look now and then in one of my old journals, though, I find that what I wrote at the time does not always correspond with the way I remember certain events. Something has happened in the intervening years. My mind has somehow altered its perception of what happened. The second limiting factor is that we do not know the present. And if we do not know the present, then our memory is filled with faded bits and pieces of something other than reality—or "things as they really are."

"We don't know the present?" you might ask. No, we don't. Anyone who has ever talked to another human being should know that no two people see the world in just the same way. That's why we have disagreements. We see things differently.

Each person has a unique personal perspective on what goes on around him or her, and that perspective is limited by one of the constraints placed on all mortals: we can focus on only one thing at a time. Our view of the present is colored by what we choose to bring into the foreground of thought, and our perception can be shaded by anything from what we ate for breakfast to whether or not we are in love. Beyond this, how we perceive life is largely a function of our most cherished beliefs and prejudices, some of which we don't even know exist.

Our view of the present definitely cannot be considered a complete comprehension of reality. We do not know everything that is happening around us. All we know is our limited perception of the few things we are able to alternatingly focus on during any given interval. And that is what goes into memory. This fact should be a warning to us about insisting that the way we see things is the only right way. We don't know what other people are seeing, what they are feeling, and who they are. The world may look very different to someone else, and the other person's perception may be just as valid as ours.

So, we do not know past, present, or future—not in the sense that God does. I think it safe to say that God experiences life far differently than we do. In fact, we cannot even imagine what reality must look like to him. He sees the sparrow fall and numbers the hairs of our heads and knows all our thoughts and feelings— at every instant. We don't really understand the meaning of the word *omniscient*. How could we without having experienced it? We find it incredible that God can know the future, but even more incredible is the notion that he can know everything at the present moment. There is no limit to his awareness of his surroundings. At any given instant God knows not only everything that is happening, but he also knows everything that has ever happened and everything that will happen, for eternities without end. That is eternal life—the fact that God experiences and comprehends an eternity in any given instant—something we cannot even imagine. Eternal life is not merely a life of endless duration, it is a particular quality of life that is eternal or infinite in its very nature.

Dimensions

The fact that God is omniscient has something to do with the way he exists in time. He knows past, present, and future. How? Well, he hasn't told us. But he has given us some information, and we can deduce some things.

Earlier in my life I thought God's knowledge of the future was a predictive sort of knowledge. In other words, God knows what I will do next Wednesday at 4 p.m. because through our lengthy premortal association and his observation of me in mortality, he knows me perfectly, he knows everyone else perfectly, and he knows how the elements will respond to the various forces that act upon them. And because of all this knowledge, he can account for all variability and randomness and can predict perfectly what I will do. This theory has obvious limitations, the most significant being that it is not true. God does not predict the future. He sees it. It is present before him. He even tells us so: "The Lord your God . . . knoweth all things, for all things are present before mine eyes" (D&C 38:1-2). Elder Neal A. Maxwell has said: "God does not live in the dimension of time as do we. Moreover, since 'all things are present with' God, his is not simply a predicting based solely upon the past. In ways which are not clear to us, he actually sees, rather than foresees, the future—because all things are, at once, present, before him!"[2]

After I understood this, I assumed that God was outside of time—that the river of time flowed on, but did not take God with it. He just sat on the bank and watched it as an outside spectator. But then I read these words of Orson Pratt: "The true God exists both in time and in space, and has as much relation to them as man or any other being. He has extension, and form, and dimensions, as well as man. He occupies space; has a body, parts and passions; can go from place to place—can eat, drink, and talk, as well as man."[3] Now, this presented me with a dilemma. How was I to reconcile this statement with that of Elder Maxwell?

What Orson Pratt said makes sense. If we imagine a God who is outside of time, then from our perspective he would be everywhere at once, and he would also be in one place for eternity, and we could even say he would be everywhere at all times. He would fill the immensity of space and yet dwell in our hearts. He would be, by definition, the God of modern Christianity who, the prophets have insisted, does not, cannot exist. The key, I believe, lies in Elder Maxwell's words, "God does not live in the dimension of time *as do we*." He inhabits time, but differently than we do. When I understood this, several things began to make sense.

How do we live in time? Time for us is one-dimensional, and it runs from past to future. The fact that time is one-dimensional for us explains our inability to know past, present, or future. What is the present to us? It is, I argue, completely empty. If we were to stop time and analyze what is going on, we would be looking at something very similar to a three-dimensional snapshot. Objects, including human beings, would be present—because of three-dimensional space—but everything would be motionless. And if we could look into a person's mind and examine the thoughts he is thinking, his mind, I suggest, would be empty. In one instant we don't think anything. Our consciousness, our ability to think, is directly related to our walk through time. Our awareness of life is much like a movie. Each succeeding instant along our one-dimensional time-line is like an individual frame of that movie. And only as the frames advance do we see motion or activity, including mental activity. We are aware of our surroundings and our own thoughts because the reel of time is unwinding. This is why we can focus on only one thing at a time—because each instant in time is virtually fixed or stationary for us. And if from instant to instant our attention shifts (which it obviously doesn't), we still would only entertain one idea at a time.

But consider the possibilities of two-dimensional time. What if every frame of our mortal movie were filled with an infinite amount of thought? Perhaps objects, including people, wouldn't move, but if a person lived in two-dimensional time, she would be able to think and feel infinitely in that one instant. Imagine the depth of experience, how full life would be. Life would begin to take on a more complete shape. We would literally be able to focus on an infinite number of things at once. We would have the leisure to count the hairs on an infinite number of heads or watch sparrows fall—if the heads and sparrows were within our immediate view. But two-dimensional time also has its limitations. Those limitations deal with seeing the past and future.

So, let's imagine three-dimensional time. This is extremely difficult, akin to imagining four-dimensional space. But let's draw a parallel. Think of one-dimensional space, a concept popular in introductory geometry classes. If space were one-dimensional, we would be unable to see anything, assuming we could exist at all. Our whole universe would lie along an infinitely long, infinitely narrow line. If space were one-dimensional, we would not be able to see ahead or behind, to the right or left, up or down. This is why we cannot see past and future. *Time for us has no substance.* It is only directional. We have a sense of moving forward and a sense of where we have been, but we cannot see past or future.

Two-dimensional space has similar limitations. Objects would have depth and width, but no height. Or they would have height and width, but no depth. Any way you look at it, with only two dimensions we would still be unable to see anything, really, because all of existence would lie on the insubstantial plane of two-dimensional space. In order to see with our eyes (or to have eyes at all), we need three dimensions of space. Now imagine three dimensions of time, in which (for God) each instant along our one mortal time line is actually infinitely high and infinitely wide. God, being wherever he is, would simply be able to look ahead or behind and actually see things as they really were, or as they really will be, since time would have substance, and not just direction.

Let's look at this from another angle. In one-dimensional time, as discussed, each moment is virtually empty. Thought and awareness are a sequential experience. In two-dimensional time, however, a person would be able to either consider one object in infinite detail or consider all things for an instant. If you inhabited two-dimensional time, you could perhaps number all the hairs on one head in an instant of our time, or count all the stars in the sky, but not both simultaneously. In order to see and comprehend all of eternity—past, present, and future—you would have to inhabit three-dimensional time. Then you would not only have "time" to count all the stars in the sky, but you could spend a literal eternity on an infinite number of objects or activities. You could watch a million sparrows fall, number the hairs on all the heads in the universe, count all the stars in the sky, hear and answer the prayers of all your children, and still have an infinite awareness of everything else in the universe. This is what it means to be omniscient, and it is far beyond our comprehension.

When God tell us "the heavens . . . cannot be numbered unto man" (Moses 1:37), he is speaking literally. If I count two numbers each second for 80 years, I will make it all the way to 2,533,880,000—roughly two-and-a-half billion. I literally don't have time to count all of God's creations. "But they are numbered unto me," he says. He has all the time in the universe to keep track of what He has created, a comforting thought for his children, by far the most important of his creations.

The Mortal Test

This explanation of how God sees past, present, and future is by no means doctrine, but it is the best explanation I can find for what we know of our eternal Father. He is not limited to focusing on one thing at a time. He can grasp all of eternity at any instant. This suggests multiple time dimensions. But why are we limited to one-dimensional time, to thinking one thought and focusing on one idea to the exclusion of all others? Hugh Nibley gives us an answer to this question.

> But why this crippling limitation on our thoughts if we are God's children? It is precisely this limitation which is the essence of our mortal existence. If every choice I make express-es a preference; if the world I build up is the world I really love and want, then with every choice I am judging myself, pro-claiming all the day long to God, angels and my fellowmen where my real values lie, where my treasure is, the things to which I give supreme importance. Hence, in this life every moment provides a perfect and foolproof test of your real char-acter, making this life a time of testing and probation.[4]

It is our one-dimensional experience that provides our test. We must constantly choose what we will think about. Sometimes we don't choose at all, or so we suppose. We let our minds wander. We switch over to autopilot. Yet this is also a choice. Most often our thoughts follow the course of habit. We don't direct them, for that takes effort. But isn't that what Joseph Smith said about faith? "When a man works by faith he works by mental exertion instead of physical force."[5] As the scriptures remind us, we will be judged by what we think, and by what we fail to think.

If we had complete comprehension of reality, as God has, it would negate the purpose of our mortal probation. Now and then, however, God has given certain mortals very limited glimpses of his perspective, and their accounts are enlightening. Moses was shown the earth, "even all of it, and there was not a particle of it which he did not behold, discerning it by the spirit of God. And he beheld also the inhabitants thereof, and there was not a soul which he beheld not; . . . and their numbers were great, even numberless as the sand upon the sea shore" (Moses 1:27-28). One instant for Moses was filled with such immense detail.

Dr. George Ritchie writes of a similar expansion of mental capacity when he was out of his body. In the presence of the radiant being, who he understood was the Son of God, he viewed his entire life. "Everything that had ever happened to me was simply there, in full view, contemporary and current, all seemingly taking place at that moment."[6]

Communication

One of the necessary limitations of one-dimensional time is the fact that we cannot fully communicate with others. Because we perceive the world around us in a personal, unique, selective, and one-dimensional manner, it is impossible for us to truly communicate what we have experienced to another person. We are very much isolated from each other.

Have you ever tried telling someone about an experience that is very important to you? Inevitably, no matter how attentively he or she listens, the other person will not comprehend the full meaning of the experience. Hence, the trite and disappointing phrase, "You had to be there." Yes, in order to truly understand what another person is trying to tell you, you would have needed to be there—not just standing next to that person, but standing inside his or her mind and soul, looking out through his or her eyes. We cannot do that. But God can.

Even when two people experience something together, their perceptions of that experience will not match. I have tried talking, for instance, with old friends about things we experienced together. I find that we not only felt different things, but we remember the experiences differently. What a certain experience meant to me is not at all what it meant to my friend. We can talk about it, but ultimately our experiences are our own—to ponder, to cherish, to remember, to be molded by, but not to share, not completely, not yet.

There is an explanation for this barrier to communication. In this life we communicate through symbols. The words on this page are symbols. If I write "chair," you translate that symbol into whatever you understand a chair to be—and it may look vastly different from the chair I envisioned when I wrote the symbol. If I write "passion" or "prejudice," you and I have an even more difficult time envisioning the same idea. So we use more words, more symbols—modifiers and adjectives and explanatory phrases—to increase understanding. When we speak, we use even more symbols, for we can add to the phonic symbols such things as body language and intonation. But all these are still symbols, pale reflections of what we really feel and wish to communicate.

Our whole existence is cluttered with symbols, which we use to try to tell people who we are, what we are thinking, and what we have experienced. We have status symbols—cars and homes and occupations and clothes and jewelry and perfumes and even haircuts—which we often use to try to define ourselves, to make a statement about our identities. We use other symbols—words and actions and expressions—to build feeble bridges between ourselves and others. But often people will translate our symbolic statements differently than we intended. Such is the danger of superficial communication. It is imperfect and can lead to false judgments. This is perhaps one reason God warned us to judge wisely.

But there is a deeper level of communication. It is spiritual, and it is more accurate. God can communicate directly to our minds through the Spirit. When this happens, there is no misunderstanding. I recall an experience I had in the mission field. My companion and I were teaching a woman one day when a very powerful spiritual presence filled the room. To me the message was a witness of the truth, a communication I could not have misunderstood. But later this woman confessed to us that the Spirit had told her on that occasion to repent. She had been a doubter, and the message to her was as personalized as it had been to me.

Years later, when my wife was in the middle of a problem pregnancy, I pleaded with the Lord for a certain understanding so that I would know what to say in a priesthood blessing I was preparing to give her and the unborn child. The Spirit whispered to my soul that this child was going to survive and in time be just fine, so that is what I promised in the blessing. There was no way medical science could have known or promised this—in fact, the night Troy was born, three months premature, the doctor in the newborn ICU told me he wouldn't make it—but the Spirit had communicated specific knowledge to me. It was not just a high probability, it was a certainty. As I write, Troy is now a healthy, intelligent first-grader.

Most Latter-day Saints have experienced this perfect and symbolless communication from on high. It is called revelation. It is almost always nonverbal, it comes quietly to the heart when we are prepared to receive it, and it is always certain. It is a language beyond the limiting symbols of our mortal communication.

People who have had what we call "out of the body" experiences relate that all communication is nonverbal when the body is not present. One account I was reading recently told how the man whose spirit left his body during a medical emergency saw three other beings in the room. One, he said, was a prostitute. Her spirit communicated that to him. It was as if he could read it in her. Dr. Ritchie says this about his own experience:

> The instant I perceived [the radiant being], a command formed itself in my mind. "Stand up!" The words came from inside me, yet they had an authority my mere thoughts had never had. I got to my feet, and as I did came the stupendous certainty: "You are in the presence of the Son of God."
>
> Again, the concept seemed to form itself inside me, but not as thought or speculation. It was a kind of knowing, immediate and complete. I knew other facts about Him too. One, that this was the most totally male Being I had ever met. . . .
>
> Above all, with that same mysterious inner certainty, I knew that this Man loved me. Far more even than power, what emanated from this Presence was unconditional love. An astonishing love. A love beyond my wildest imagining. This love

knew every unlovable thing about me—the quarrels with my stepmother, my explosive temper, the sex thoughts I could never control, every mean, selfish thought and action since the day I was born—and accepted and loved me just the same.[7]

There is, I believe, in the eternal realms, a kind of communication that goes far beyond symbols. It is a communication of feeling, of thought, of being, of self. It is a kind of communication that will enable us to share in perfect and complete intimacy all that we could ever wish for another soul to understand about us. The reason I believe this is that God already understands us in this complete manner. The only reason our Heavenly Father can judge us is that he understands us. His perfect and complete knowledge of the universe includes the knowledge of who we are.

In some way that we cannot understand, he knows us. He sees through our eyes, feels our emotions, understands our motives, and comprehends our faulty perception of our circumstances. If it were not so, he would be unable to judge us. If he were merely an outside observer, he would not qualify. But he is not limited to merely viewing our actions, as, I might add, Satan is. God knows our thoughts and attitudes and the intents of our hearts—as if they were his own. It is because he does know us better than we know ourselves that he can judge us. And he judges us with love. He is not a vindictive, cynical Peeping Tom, who laughs at what he sees. He is a merciful, loving Father, whose infinite powers are focused on saving our souls without encroaching upon our eternal agency. And someday, if we choose well in this life, we will be able to be the same kind of loving, understanding parents to our spirit children.

4

Fallen Man

Essential to our search for identity is an understanding of the relationship between body and spirit. And here we must distinguish between actual present identity and potential identity. Potential identity, or destiny, is what we ultimately can become if we fulfill the end of our creation. But that potential identity is usually a far cry from our present identity, what we actually are, for what we are is an odd conglomeration of good intentions, righteous acts, nagging weaknesses, recurring sins, sporadic intelligence, abundant ignorance, arbitrary prejudices, alternating zeal and indifference, hidden strengths, and powerful urges, all held together by a unique sense of personality. We have, as David O. McKay taught, a dual nature,

> one related to the earthly or animal life, the other, akin to the divine. Whether a man remains satisfied within what we designate the animal world, satisfied with what the animal world will give him, yielding without effort to the whim of his appetites

and passions and slipping farther and farther into the realm of indulgence, or whether through self-mastery, he rises toward intellectual, moral, and spiritual enjoyments depends upon the kind of choice he makes every day, every hour of his life.[1]

The world, especially the world of behavioral science, would have us believe that our true identity is nothing more than some composite of the myriad urges, instincts, and passions that come as standard equipment in the body. But the body is inhabited by a spirit, and that spirit is guided by an intelligence. Although the spirit is not perfect and is still plagued by various weaknesses, it comes to earth innocent and yearns initially for things that are good and right and pure. The spirit comes from the presence of God, and, although it cannot remember its former life, it has a sort of homing device that attracts it to spiritual things. And this places it in conflict with the body, for the body is fallen, is earthly, and is burdened with urges and passions that pull us, as President McKay explained, toward the animal world.

This inner conflict, which I call the mortal conflict, pulls us in two directions and sets up a struggle between our true eternal identity and a temporal, fallen identity. Consequently, as we exercise free agency, our choices either bring us closer to our true identity or draw us further from it. If we make wrong choices, our present identity becomes something less noble than what our potential indicates it should be.

Cars and Drivers

When I was a young boy of maybe four or five years, my grandfather would take me for rides in his car. He would find a road in the sparsely populated community where he lived, and there he would let me "drive the car." I couldn't see over the dash board, my feet didn't reach the gas and brake pedals, and the steering wheel was a bit too large and stiff for me to turn. Fortunately, Grandpa was there next to me to help me steer and to push on the accelerator and the brake. I can imagine what might have happened had he not been there by my side. Grandpa's old Dodge, I suppose, would have pretty well driven itself—contrary to its name—into trees, rocks, people, or anything that stood in its path.

The inevitable analogy here is that we mortals are very much like Grandpa's old car. Each of us has a spirit driver that has been placed in an earthly vehicle of flesh and blood. When the spirit has grown mature enough to control the body, everything is fine, and the body does what it should do. If for some reason, though, the spirit cannot prevent the body from following its own impulses, then great sorrow and harm can come to us and to those around us.

Sometimes the spirit is seemingly asleep at the wheel, lost in a spiritual slumber, and the body is left to drive itself. Sometimes the spirit becomes diseased or injured (with sin) and does not respond as it should, and it cannot control the body. Sometimes the spirit is drugged or intoxicated (perhaps with pride and ambition), and even though it tries to pursue what it sees as a worthy course, its vision is blurred and distorted. In still other instances, the spirit apparently remains a child, immature, and finds itself in a body with urges and desires and powers too strong for it to control. But whatever the reason, if the body governs the spirit, we call that condition "the natural man," and the soul (the union of body and spirit) loses agency. Whenever a soul loses agency, its eternal identity is diminished, for it then lacks full power of expression.

An Enemy to God

King Benjamin taught that "the natural man is an enemy to God" (Mosiah 3:19). Does this mean that Satan has such total control over the individual that he openly opposes the work of the Lord? Not necessarily.

> What does it mean to be an enemy to God? Does it mean that a man . . . finds himself in open conflict, pursuing things that are unrighteous, living [a life] of depravity? . . . I'm reasonably sure that's not what King Benjamin is talking about. There is a point, however, where we sense our allegiance running to the world instead of . . . to the Savior or to things spiritual. . . . One finds himself in conflict. If that conflict with things of the world . . . becomes sufficiently strong [and] we find ourselves laboring with compromise, arguing with self, and making decisions contrary to the mind and will of God, running in the face of his commandments, his revealed mind and will—at that point we find ourselves at enmity with divine things.[2]

So, we can be unintentional, unwitting enemies. Whenever we find ourselves at enmity with divine things, including our own eternal identity, our potential, we are enemies to God. "The natural man" says King Benjamin, "is an enemy to God, *and has been from the fall of Adam*" (Mosiah 3:19, italics mine). This last phrase is especially significant.

The Fall of Adam

Among Christians, a too common attitude toward the fall of Adam is that it was not literal and that the Garden of Eden was only symbolic, as were the two central trees in the Garden. Some even doubt the existence of Adam and Eve. But an even more common attitude is that of indifference. "Who cares anyway what happened in the Garden? That was long ago and doesn't really apply to my life today." But the Garden was real, and Adam and Eve did exist, and what happened there so long ago has a very intimate meaning for each of us, for by understanding Adam, we come to understand our Father better, and we come to understand ourselves.

What were Adam and Eve like before the fall? The Sunday School answer is, of course, that they couldn't sin because they didn't know good from evil, they were unable to have children, they were in the presence of God, and so forth. But *why* didn't they know good and evil, *why* were they unable to have children, and *why* were they cast out of God's presence? These are the questions we should ask.

We often think of Adam and Eve before the fall as, essentially, children. But they were like children in only a limited sense. They were intelligent, able to walk and talk with God, able to be instructed. But for some reason their understanding lacked something—something they would gain by partaking of the forbidden fruit, something they had partially possessed in the pre-existence. Adam and Eve had been made innocent again when they were sent into the Garden. Any sins they may have committed in the pre-existence had been forgiven, and they were pure. But something else had been taken from them—the ability to commit sin.

In order to commit sin a person must be able to make knowledgable choices, and in order to make knowledgable choices a person must understand the difference between alternatives and opposites. In certain ways Adam and Eve could not recognize opposition—most particularly the opposition that occurs within the heart of each mortal. And because of this, they were unable to have certain experiences. They could feel neither anger nor compassion, patience nor impatience, lust nor love, mercy nor malevolence, envy nor empathy. It was as if a veil had been cast over their immortal spirits, limiting what they could experience. These emotions, and the actions that naturally follow such emotions, were impossible—until something changed in their bodies.

That change was caused by their partaking of the forbidden fruit. Before the fall, the bodies of Adam and Eve differed from our bodies. Says President Joseph Fielding Smith: "When Adam and Eve were placed in the Garden of Eden, there was no blood in their bodies. Their lives were quickened by spirit; therefore they were in a state where they could have lived forever."[3]

Apparently, when Adam and Eve partook of the forbidden fruit, blood began to flow in their veins, and not only did this cause mortality to come upon them, but with that change came the unleashing of passions and powers in the physical body. And these passions and powers, which we have inherited through the fall, endow us with a full spectrum of emotion or, if you will, inner experience, inner opposition.

The presence of these passions is essential to our eternal progress, for without them and the inner opposition they supply, we would, in a manner of speaking, have no existence—at least not in the fullest sense of the word. We would hardly be alive. In certain respects we would be "things of naught," to use Lehi's expression, unable to distinguish between lust and love or mercy and malice—and, more significantly, unable to choose between them—which is why God did not want Adam and Eve to continue in that condition. Had they remained in their innocent, prefall state, they would have been damned. But they stepped onto the path of agency, and by so doing opened that road for us also. And these forces of inner opposition that we have inherited through the fall help us define our identities. Since we know both the fire of anger and the whisperings of compassion, we are able choose between them and thereby determine what kind of individuals we will become.

Inner Opposition

In essence, these oppositional passions or internal experiences are among the most important powers of godhood, for God is a being with body, parts, and passions. It is the choices we make as these passions exert themselves that lead us toward either exaltation or eternal damnation. But the passions, in and of themselves, are not evil. Each passion comes with bounds and limits, beyond which they do us harm. Their lawful use can take us on a straight course to freedom and perfection, but just as a driver who disregards traffic laws and signals will inevitably cause injury or death, so will a soul who disregards the limits and laws placed upon the use of the body and its passions cause spiritual misery or death.

Love, for instance, can be either good or evil. It contains its own opposition. If we love the Lord with all our heart and love our neighbors, that is good. But if we love money or idols or Satan, that is evil. What we love is important, for our choice shapes our identity. But how we love is equally significant. If this passion gets out of control, it can become anything from jealousy or possessiveness to lust.

Anger has similar bounds. If we focus our anger on sin and wickedness, as does God, and not turn it toward our fellowmen, we are being Christlike. Mercy, usually thought of as good and desirable, can become something less so if it crosses its necessary boundary and becomes permissiveness or indifference.

The passions are not evil except when the spirit is not strong enough to govern them and restrict them to their lawful use. Therefore, the weaknesses of each individual spirit are important. We must seek to know our innate spiritual makeup, discover the weaknesses we have brought with us, so that we can overcome them. And mortality is specifically designed to help us identify those weaknesses. The passions of mortality illuminate our weak spots. The passionless life in the Garden, by contrast, was not conducive to such fundamental discoveries.

Before the fall, Adam and Eve were like God in that they were immortal and pure; but they were unlike God in that they were empty of passion and were not perfect. Adam and Eve were innocent but imperfect. Perfection lies in governing the passions of the flesh and in identifying and overcoming the weaknesses inherent in the spirit. The process of attaining perfection is largely the mending of the inner rift or mortal conflict I mentioned earlier—the conflict between body and spirit. This is the true business of mortality.

A Parallel

Our lives reflect the fall of Adam and Eve almost exactly. Our spirits come from the premortal world completely innocent. And that is an interesting thought. We know that we had weaknesses and that there was sin in the pre-existence. We know that the atonement was in force and that we were able to repent of our sins. But if we come into mortality pure and innocent (see D&C 93:38), we must have done something to become so.

The scriptures draw parallels between baptism and birth. Moses 6:59 teaches us of the presence of water, blood, and spirit in each. We come forth from the baptismal font to new life and take upon us a new name, just as we do in birth. But the most forgotten parallel between the two is that we are made innocent after both baptism and birth. We could easily assume that birth is more than just an entrance into mortality. It may very well be an ordinance, for we know that it invokes the powers of the atonement in our behalf. We are made clean when we are born into this world and pass through the veil, or enter into the flesh.

As children we are very similar to Adam and Eve before the fall. We cannot sin, because our understanding of the opposition within ourselves is incomplete and the passions of the flesh are not fully awakened. It is as if they slumber. But when we reach a certain stage in our maturity, something changes. We become fully accountable for our actions. A conflict then arises between the untamed, fallen flesh and the spirit, and battle lines are drawn. Then, to complicate matters, as we become increasingly aware of the world around us, its allures and temptations impinge upon us and work upon the passions that have awakened within the flesh.

When our full faculties are aroused, the weaknesses in the spirit become evident as we discover which internal passions and which attractions of the world are most difficult for us to master. Some people give in to the craving of the flesh for substances that create exciting or addicting sensations—narcotics, alcohol, tobacco, caffeine. Sexual temptations are closely akin to this craving. Malice, impatience, jealousy, indolence, apathy, and selfishness all consist of giving in to either the passions or passiveness of the flesh and not remaining within the Lord's prescribed limits. The body is also drawn by the material world around us. Stealing, deceit, covetousness, vanity, refusing to pay tithes and offerings, and breaking the Sabbath are all signs of the pull of the world on the flesh and either our inability or lack of desire to resist.

The real conflict, however, is not between us and the world—the conflict is within us. Contact with the world is simply unavoidable, and the world's evils attract certain sensitive spots in us, like a magnet attracts steel. The mortal conflict, however, is between the spirit, which comes from the presence of God and hungers for spiritual things, and the fallen flesh, which yearns to unleash its passions from any limits or restraints. Indulgence and instant gratification are what the body seeks, not controlled application of the passions in a quest for the abundant life. The crucial question of mortality is whether we have the strength of spirit to turn a deaf ear to these unlawful yearnings and desires (as Satan plays upon them), or whether we give in to the passiveness and passions of carnality and slip into behaviors that are at enmity with our eternal identity.

Desires

The message of the gospel is *not* that we have no choice but to surrender to our weaknesses, to give in to the yearnings of the flesh. Weakness may constitute a part of our present spiritual makeup. We may have deficiencies that we brought with us from the pre-existence. Our spirits were not perfect there, nor are they here. But our weaknesses, whatever they may be, are not part of our eternal potential identity—our destiny. We have agency, and we can change. We can initiate the process by which our weaknesses are transformed into strengths, our present imperfect reality into our ultimate perfection.

The real test in mortality is a test of our desires, for the desires of our hearts will ultimately dictate our choices. And individual desires are, well, individual, but they are also both intricate and influential. Our desires, more than perhaps any other factor, make us what we are—and what we will become. If we truly want to reach our ultimate potential and become gods, no power this side of heaven can thwart us, and no power in heaven will resist us. If our desires are right, we will search out our spiritual weaknesses, implore heaven for the spiritual power to govern the flesh, and, recognizing the marvelous opposition created within us by the passions we have inherited, we will choose in our own unique way to honor the bounds the Lord has prescribed for exercising those passions.

5

The Gospel of Behaviorism

Reshaping and reforming our present, fallen identity so that it comes into harmony with our eternal, potential identity requires the peaceful though not passive settling of the mortal conflict. This involves identifying and, through the grace of God, overcoming weaknesses in the spirit and purifying the flesh. This process is known by several names—forgiveness, spiritual rebirth, sanctification.

As I suggested earlier, sin is something more than just bad behavior. There are more fundamental forces at work. Sometimes sin results when the spirit is too weak to govern the flesh. At other times the spirit wilfully rebels and follows the body's lead. And in some instances the spirit is confused or overwhelmed by the new experiences and sensations of this physical world. But whatever the exact case may be, what we usually call sin is merely the behavioral manifestation of a deeper, more fundamental conflict. For this reason, repentance must be more than just a behavioral Band-Aid.

The Merry-Go-Round of Repentance

So, what exactly does it mean to repent? That question sounds fairly simple, until we look at it in the context of real life. Then it becomes more problematic. Most Latter-day Saints could list the four or five or six steps of repentance. I can't even remember how many there are, let alone what they are, because in my own life, at a very personal level, I have never been able to see repentance as something similar to putting a bicycle together—you know, Step 1, Step 2, Step 3.

But I do know this. Many of us are frustrated by weaknesses that we just can't seem to get the best of. We recognize the sin and are genuinely sorry for our behavior; we confess and make restitution, but it all breaks down at the point of forsaking the sin. In my own case, just about when I think I've got my impatience licked, someone pulls in front of me on a two-lane highway and drives twenty miles an hour under the speed limit, and before I know it, I'm ready to blast away on the horn, my blood pressure rises, I've thought up several imaginative and descriptive names for "that idiot driver"—and suddenly I'm back to square one.

This, then, to me is the crux of repentance and forgiveness: "Behold he who has repented of his sins, the same is forgiven, and I, the Lord, remember them no more. By this ye may know if a man repenteth of his sins—behold, he will confess them and forsake them" (D&C 58:42-43). Confessing is often hard, but all it usually takes is a little courage. Forsaking, on the other hand, sometimes seems impossible. "I was born that way. I inherited my temper from my Irish grandfather. I can't change. I've tried. It doesn't work." Or so we sometimes rationalize.

Have you ever felt frustrated because you struggle with the same weakness over and over and over—the spirit gains control of the body for a few days, then loses it? Well, join the club. After considering the scriptures and my own life, I've come to the conclusion that there are two very distinct levels of repentance. One I call *repentance according to the Gospel of Behaviorism*. It is nothing more than behavior modification. Reinforce good behavior and suppress bad behavior. Its goal is to create good habits. And so instead of purity and spiritual vitality, we end up with the stereotypical "Mormon lifestyle," whatever that is, and live our lives in a state of mindless conformance (I refuse to use the term obedience for this condition) that is not exactly bad, but is definitely not sanctifying—it has no power to bring our souls within reach of Christ's power.

The premise of the Gospel of Behaviorism is that behavior is nothing more than a response to external stimuli—that human beings are no different from Pavlov's dogs. It assumes that by changing behavior, you can solve every problem an individual might have and eliminate his or her weaknesses. This approach has been used widely to treat alcohol and drug addictions, has found popular application in weight-loss programs, and has even been suggested as a way of casting out impure thoughts. You remember—when an evil thought comes, hum your favorite hymn. Introduce a positive stimulus. Now, I'm not saying this approach is bad. I am merely saying it may be inadequate. Whatever form it takes, behavior modification's emphasis is on behavior, on the symptom.

I may notice, for example, that I am particularly impatient with slow or incompetent drivers. And I may make a conscious effort to show patience when driving behind them. I may devise a system to reinforce positive behavior. For instance, when someone pulls out in front of me on the highway and drives slowly, I may train myself to think of that person as my aged grandfather or grandmother, whose reflexes have slowed with the years and should never drive as fast as I tend to. I might even tape a picture of my grandmother on the windshield to remind me to think these thoughts. This approach is not bad. It may even curb my driving behavior. The point, however, is that this is behaviorism. I have created a new external stimulus to change my behavior in one particular instance. When the bell rings, I salivate. But this little ritual would do nothing to conquer the underlying weakness. In other words, the root of impatience is not impatient behavior. The real root will send out runners and sprout proof of its persistence in a hundred different corners of my behavioral garden. If I want to be rid of the weakness, I must dig it up by the root. This implies a deep and basic understanding of who I am, including my weaknesses, and who I can become.

Trying to forsake certain sins by focusing on behavior is somewhat like trying to make autumn come by pulling all the leaves off the trees. The leaves of sin will fall only when a more fundamental change occurs, for sin is a consequence, a symptom of a more basic problem. Even if we do modify our behavior, the weakness, the inherent flaw in our spiritual makeup that allows the body to control the spirit, the source of the sin, may persist and may manifest itself in other ways. I would suggest that repentance based on behavior modification is not true repentance at all, because it ignores the heart, core, and primary moving principle of the gospel—faith in Jesus Christ.

I have had the unfortunate blessing to have participated, as a member of both a bishopric and a high council, in nearly twenty church courts. I bring up this sad fact only because the majority of these courts were convened for repeat transgressions of the law of chastity. These people thought they had their weakness licked. The first time around their sorrow had been sincere, they had confessed and sincerely tried to forsake the sin, but as time passed they found that, like a spiritual merry-go-round, they had come full circle and were right back where they had been a year or two earlier. In terms of pain and remorse, they had logged many miles, but spiritually speaking, they had gotten nowhere. Such is the carousel of behavioristic repentance.

Reason tells us that to truly overcome the cause of sin—to step off the behavioristic merry-go-round—either the body must be purified, purged of its fallen nature, or the spirit must be strengthened, so that it can govern the body. These are the only possible paths to resolving the mortal conflict. Fortunately, the two usually happen simultaneously.

The unspoken truth about behavioristic "repentance" is that, at best, it makes us honorable men and women of the earth. In other words, it will land us in the upper realms of the terrestrial kingdom. The Gospel of Jesus Christ, on the other hand, points us to a higher level of existence, a level not reachable by either the Ben Franklin approach to perfection or any number of self-improvement programs. Sanctification lies beyond our natural levels of performance. It is a perfection that comes through the atonement of Christ.

Unspoken Assumptions

Some implicit assumptions burden the behavioristic approach to repentance. First, that man *is* his behavior. I am what I do. If I can change what I do, I change what I am. Second, that man has no innate human nature. I am neither good nor bad, only potential. I am whatever my environment makes me, therefore, I am not responsible for what I am; the world around me is responsible. And third, that creating good habits will create perfect people. It doesn't matter what I think and feel, as long as I don't act on those feelings.

These assumptions, of course, are incorrect. Man is much more than his behavior—he is a complex being of desires and attitudes and motives. And changing behavior does not necessarily change these inner aspects of individual identity. Even if I can somehow reshape my behavior, I may still hold attitudes or entertain thoughts that I don't dare reveal, perhaps because of social pressure or others' opinions. I may even develop good behavioral patterns for selfish or immoral reasons. I may curb my behavior, for instance, because of personal pride or vain ambition or merely because I want to impress someone. Motivation and purpose are at least as important as raw behavior. In short, I can change my behavior without changing my nature.

And I do believe there is such a thing as innate human nature. Men and women, I argue, are basically good—their desires, at least when they arrive in mortality, are fundamentally right. "But what about Satan?" you ask. "If he existed from eternity, as you insist, as a distinct personality with agency, wasn't he more bad than good?" That is a good question. But I imagine that originally even Satan was basically good. His weaknesses merely caught up with him and his untamed desires consumed him—because he gave in to them. His choices reflect this. He decided, with full accountability and sufficient knowledge of the consequences, to step beyond prescribed boundaries. This stripped all goodness from him, leaving him totally, eternally corrupt.

We read in the Doctrine and Covenants: "Every spirit of man was innocent in the beginning; and God having redeemed man from the fall, men became *again, in their infant state,* innocent before God" (D&C 93:38, italics added). We have already discussed the fact that we are made pure and innocent again at our mortal birth. The key word is "again." We were innocent once before—in the beginning. The word "beginning" here must refer to the beginning of our existence as spirit children of God. And this makes good sense. If we existed as intelligences, as individual personalities with agency, before our spirit birth, I think it safe to assume that before God would give us spirit bodies and set us on the path toward godhood, he would require us to make certain decisions and perhaps covenants. It also makes good sense that we were not forced into our spirit bodies any more than we were forced into our physical bodies, but rather, that we had the choice to accept the Father's plan and become his spirit children. That step, like every other step in our progression, was undoubtedly governed by certain requirements, perhaps even covenants. So we were apparently made innocent at our spirit birth, as a consequence of our choices.

Satan, I would argue, was basically good, at least good enough to be given a spirit body and made innocent. He undoubtedly had severe weaknesses woven into his innermost desires that manifested themselves as he received power and authority and was placed in a position to more fully exercise his agency. His choices eventually changed his identity, staining him from white to black. He chose to deny his ultimate destiny as a child of God. Instead of desiring to become like God, he wanted to replace God.

We were also basically good in our first estate, and apparently we were strong enough to choose correctly. We chose to take the next step in our progression. We accepted the Savior and came to earth and were made innocent again. But even though we were made innocent, we retained certain weaknesses. Those weaknesses now manifest themselves in our everyday lives, and it is the grand struggle of mortality for us to come to terms with those weaknesses and eradicate them. Our choices in mortality will determine whether our basic goodness endures and becomes perfect or atrophies into any of several degrees of evil. Regardless of our ultimate choices in this life, however, in order to have made it this far in our progression, we all must have had a high degree of intrinsic goodness in us from the beginning.

The third assumption of behaviorism, that creating good habits will create good people, is also flawed. As human beings, we are more than an accumulation of habits. We are more than mindless responses to external stimuli. We have agency. And just because we develop the habit of not committing adultery does not mean that we are not adulterous in a far more fundamental way. Jesus proclaimed a higher law, a law that encompasses even the thoughts and intents of our hearts. We must become as he is—consciously good and righteous. It is not enough to thoughtlessly mimic his actions. We must become pure in our hearts, for those who are pure by nature will be incapable of either clinging to impure motives or performing unclean acts. They will have developed *a righteous identity* that far exceeds mere habit.

Faith in Christ

We've talked about the counterfeit repentance of behaviorism, of behavioral Band-Aids. True repentance, by contrast, has only one premise—that it is not primarily our behavior but our nature that needs changing. Its focus is on the atonement of Jesus Christ. But sometimes, I believe, though our intentions are good, our faith in that atonement falls just one concept short of being effective, and as a result, what starts out as genuine repentance often ends up as temporary behavior modification.

We all know that Christ suffered for us so that we would not have to suffer. We all know that he can cleanse us of sin, make us

pure again, as if we hadn't sinned at all. But there is one capabil-
ity he has, because of the atonement, that makes all the difference in our ability to forsake sin—and it is easy to overlook this,
even though it is the central message of the Book of Mormon.
Christ has the power to change our nature. Merely wiping the
slate clean, to use the popular metaphor, is not enough. If we sin
and repent, but still bear the same weakness that caused us to sin
in the first place, we will almost certainly sin again. We will be no
better off, and we will struggle with that weakness over and over
and repent again and again—the same old merry-go-round.

Our faith in Christ is complete only when we have faith in his
ability to change us on the inside—not just change our behavior,
but change our hearts, our desires, and make us like he is. This is
the grand key of the gospel: that our desires can be sanctified, so
that we, like the people of King Benjamin "have no more disposition to do evil, but to do good continually" (Mosiah 5:2).

Sanctification doesn't always happen overnight. Sometimes it
takes time. But the fact is, Christ can lift us above sin—cleanse
and purge our flesh of its carnal tendencies, renew and strength-
en our spirits—heal the fundamental flaws that cause sin. For we
must learn to become not only innocent again, we must become
perfect. And perfection implies an overcoming of all evil desires,
all weakness and carnality, which unfortunately play too big a part
in our identity as fallen creatures.

True Repentance

True repentance involves the removal of the inner conflict
between body and spirit. It is more than trying to fool the body.
Let me illustrate. I know a man in Germany who had joined the
Church some five months before I met him. He told me one day

about his conversion. When the missionaries found him, he said, he smoked sixty to eighty cigarettes, drank one bottle of hard liquor, and consumed eight to ten cups of coffee each day. He believed all that the elders taught him and gratefully accepted their baptismal challenge. But he had one little problem—he couldn't give up his cigarettes and alcohol and coffee. It wasn't that he didn't want to. He simply couldn't. He was addicted—physically, psychologically—whatever the case, he couldn't quit. But the missionaries told him that if he had faith in Christ, if he truly believed, he could overcome this one weakness that was holding him back. Well, he believed. And overnight something inside him changed. From that day he had no more desire for alcohol, tobacco, or caffeine. No desire. Not even when he smelled the smoke of someone else's cigarette or saw others drinking—not a hint of the craving that those people experience who overcome these habits by behavior modification. Not in twenty years. He was made new, born again, you might say, in that area.

Contrast this with the account I read recently of a reporter who attempted to quit smoking. He tried every method—from chewing nicotine gum (changing the external stimulus) to hypnosis (trying to dupe the spirit). And he did quit—several times. But each time the weakness got the best of him. His spirit could only conquer the cravings of the flesh for a few months, then he was back to two packs a day. Nephi calls this approach trusting in the arm of flesh. I call it pulling the leaves off the trees. It's a twisted, inverted method.

Let me illustrate further. Latter-day Saints have been taught to hum a favorite hymn when evil thoughts assail them. This isn't bad counsel—and neither is the behavioral approach to giving up smoking. But compare this purely behavioral diversion of inappropriate thoughts with this account:

I remember the story of a man I knew at an earlier time in my life—a dear friend. One day he confided in me and said: "You know, I've had a struggle all my life with this principle of virtue. Never once have I violated the law. Never once have I committed adultery. I've been able to keep myself free from those kinds of transgressions. But there have oftentimes been thoughts and feelings come into my heart, and I've been mindful of them, and of the Savior's reference to the higher law . . . . I asked myself, would I never reach a point of being totally free of that weakness? . . . I have tried, earnestly tried, to purge my heart, to rid myself of feelings that would be inappropriate. Over the years, with fasting and prayer and much faith, I've accomplished a reformation of the inner man."

Then he said this: "I had an interesting experience a few weeks ago. I had taken my wife shopping, and as it is with some women, they enjoy shopping more than men, and men become weary before their wives. I don't know where she was getting all her energy from, but I said, 'I'm going to leave you here. You go at it. I'm going to the car to rest. I'll meet you later.' So I went to the car, . . . and as I was sitting, aimlessly thinking, a lovely young woman walked down the street in front of me. I watched her, and all of a sudden I became aware of the fact that thoughts were racing where they shouldn't have been. And I found myself full of feelings that did not belong. To me it was most alarming, because it represented an old struggle, an old battle that I thought I had long since been able to leave. It represented a battlefield, which had left me with a few scars, mostly healed. And there I found myself again in the throes of a struggle. Almost spontaneously I cried out within, 'Oh Lord, have mercy on me! Wrap me about with the robes of thy righteousness!' No sooner had I spoken those words than a power descended upon me, from the crown of my head to the soles of my feet, removing things alien and foreign and placing peace and tranquility in my heart."

Now, we can talk about that and say, "Well, isn't that quite a bit to expect from a man or a woman, to become that holy and that righteous?" I suggest to you: that is the battlefield upon which we must find ourselves. As I read the Doctrine and Covenants, we are told that the terrestrial degree of glory will be inherited by the honorable, the good, the noble men of the earth. But as I understand it, those who go to the celestial kingdom will be holy men and holy women, redeemed through the grace of Christ, given strength to overcome their weaknesses, overcoming their fallen nature by the Spirit.[1]

So who are we? We are fallen men and women. We have a spirit that comes from God's presence and yearns to return. We have a body that is enticed by the carnal and worldly influences that surround it. Who will we be? The choice is ours. The power of Christ is available to us, if we truly desire to draw upon it. He can quell the mortal conflict and perfect us by mending and reshaping our present identity into one that will naturally grow to fulfill our eternal destiny.

6

The Grand Heresy

✧⊰∞⊱✧

The pivotal truth of our entire theology is Lorenzo Snow's simple declaration: "As man now is, God once was; as God now is, man may be." This couplet declares our destiny and defines our existence as a progression from a lower station to a higher one. We came to earth because we could progress no further as spirits, and if we are successful in this stage of our eternal existence, we can lay claim upon that grandest of all destinies—godhood.

As we begin our climb toward godhood, though, our attention seems often captured by the lesser laws, and our focus is on following the letter of these laws. Pay 10 percent of your income as tithing, don't commit adultery, don't gossip, read the scriptures daily, and so on. The letter of the law focuses on the minimum requirement and is always behavior oriented. But this behavioral gospel can become mere habit—as meaningless as putting the right shoe on before the left—and it can leave us spiritually exhausted, for there is no real nourishment in habit.

The Gospel of Habit

Now, I'm not saying good habits aren't desirable. Good habits are obviously much better than bad ones. But the gospel of habit will land us in the higher regions of the terrestrial kingdom, along with all the other good and honorable and decent people of the earth. For something is missing if we allow the gospel to become meaningless ritual. Let me give an example. At times in my life I have paid tithing like an automatic teller machine—push the tithing button and out comes 10 percent. Pure reflex. It didn't hurt to give away that money—in fact, I'm embarrassed to say I didn't even think about it. And what's worse, it didn't do me much good, for I firmly believe that unless I exercise faith in offering that 10 percent, unless there is purpose behind my performance, the windows of heaven get at least partially stuck and the power of that gospel principle lies largely dormant.

I can live the gospel to the fullest minimum requirement—paint my fence, attend my meetings, refrain from smoking and drinking, obey the laws of the land, attend the temple regularly, work on the welfare farm, honor my parents, remain faithful to my wife, hold family home evening every week, shun profanity, sustain my church leaders, avoid lying and coveting and stealing, do my home teaching, pay my tithes and offerings, and a hundred other things—I can be worthy of a temple recommend—and yet still feel spiritually dead if these actions are simply habit or thoughtless ritual. Indeed, I can go through the motions of the gospel and develop a religious lifestyle, and yet never once feel in my soul the purpose of the commandments, never once catch a glimpse of the higher law, the spirit of the gospel, never once make significant progress in my attempt to become like the Son of God.

The Purpose of the Law

Fortunately, the Lord gives us some commandments—the two great commandments, to love God and neighbor, and the law of the Sabbath, for instance—that have no definite minimum requirements. Perhaps he does this to teach us to be sensitive to the spirit of the law, to entice us onward and upward. These commandments can serve as types and examples of all other laws, teaching us how to seek the purpose for which they are given. Adam, when he was first driven from the Garden of Eden, lived a behavior-oriented gospel.

> And after many days an angel of the Lord appeared unto Adam, saying: Why dost thou offer sacrifices unto the Lord? And Adam said unto him: I know not, save the Lord commanded me.
>
> And the angel spake, saying: This thing is a similitude of the sacrifice of the Only Begotten of the Father, which is full of grace and truth.
>
> Wherefore, thou shalt do all that thou doest in the name of the Son, and thou shalt repent and call upon God in the name of the Son forevermore.
>
> And in that day the Holy Ghost fell upon Adam, which beareth record of the Father and the Son, saying: I am the Only Begotten of the Father from the beginning, henceforth and forever, that as thou hast fallen thou mayest be redeemed, and all mankind, even as many as will.
>
> And in that day Adam blessed God and was filled, and began to prophesy concerning all the families of the earth. (Moses 5:6-10)

Adam obeyed at first simply because the Lord commanded it.

And this, by the way, is a very good reason to obey. But I don't believe the Lord wanted Adam (or wants us) to remain at that level permanently. It is only when we understand the purpose of our actions and our worship that we gain an understanding of the higher laws and can partake of the power of the gospel. Adam, when he was instructed regarding the purpose of his actions—when he had gained intelligence—was filled with the Holy Ghost and began to prophesy, began to receive revelation.

The Higher Laws

The important idea is that we can reach a point at which living the gospel brings power into our lives because we understand the purpose. Instead of following the letter of the law, because that is all we have, we follow the spirit. And this does not mean we just ignore the letter. Some people excuse their failure at keeping certain commandments by saying they are living the spirit of the law, when in fact they are living neither the letter nor the spirit. For the spirit of the law *encompasses* and *exceeds* the letter. It is much more inclusive, for it involves fulfilling the purpose of the law. And the higher laws are all purpose-oriented laws; they are open-ended. They do not require uniform, programmed behavior, and they have no minimum requirements. With the higher laws the specifics change constantly, depending on our circumstances; indeed, conformance may require different actions in different situations.

We not only pay tithing with faith in the Lord, understanding that tithing is a small part of the law of consecration, but we also pay a generous fast offering and look for opportunities to help those less fortunate than we are and budget our finances as if they were the Lord's.

We not only refrain from committing adultery and looking on someone else to lust after him or her, we love our husband or wife with *all* our heart (see D&C 42:22), serving, building, sustaining, comforting, and adoring him or her. How many units is *all*? *All* completely excludes minimum requirements.

When we understand the higher law, we search the scriptures, not primarily because the prophet told us to read the Book of Mormon, but because the word of God teaches us of Christ and leads us to him, and it prepares our hearts to receive instruction from him through the Holy Spirit.

And this is the key to living the higher laws, the key to becoming more like God: revelation. Even if we understand the higher laws, if left to our own devices, we would be at a loss in trying to obey with any degree of success such open-ended commandments. The higher laws are not something we can write in our ubiquitous day planners to constantly remind us what we should do. They must be written on our hearts so that we spontaneously live them as the Spirit guides us. Living the spirit of the law requires a healthy dose of heavenly assistance.

The Internal Gospel

Truly receiving the Holy Ghost represents a major step in our progress toward godhood, for it marks the point at which the gospel changes from an external gospel to an internal one. Living an external gospel means that we receive our cues from outside sources—the prophet, local Church leaders, the scriptures, parents, and teachers. These commandments and bits and pieces of counsel that make up the external gospel usually come in a very general form, often focusing on the "don'ts" of our behavior, and leave the broad spectrum of specific acts of righteousness up to us to figure out. On the other hand, living an internal gospel means that we receive our cues directly from the Spirit, in our hearts, in specifics, applicable to everyday circumstances. The Spirit teaches us how to live the higher law and reach the higher levels of obedience.

The external gospel says, "Love your neighbor as yourself." The internal gospel says, "Go visit Sister Anderson today. She's lonely." The external gospel says, "Pay your tithing." The internal gospel says, "Brother Phillips is out of work. Why don't you use some of the financial blessings you've received and anonymously support his missionary son this month?" The outward gospel says, "Not only shouldn't you commit adultery, you should love your wife with all your heart." The inward gospel says, "Your kids have worn your wife to a frazzle this week. The budget won't let you take her out to eat until after payday—so why don't you cook dinner for her. This unselfish act will strengthen your marriage." The outward gospel says, "Keep the Sabbath Day holy." The inward gospel says, "Write your grandfather a letter today. He is weary and discouraged from caring night and day for your failing grandmother. A letter would cheer him up."

You get the idea. I'm not saying that the Spirit needs to tell us everything we should do, or that we shouldn't do good deeds of our own free will. I am saying that the Spirit can prompt us and teach us to live the gospel at a higher level than we normally would be able to. It can help us to know God and what he would do if he were in our circumstances. And as we listen to the spirit of revelation and follow the promptings of the Holy Ghost, light and truth come to grow in us and become part of us, so that we will know, more and more, what we should do, and will not require as much prompting. This kind of obedience, as opposed to mindless conformance, is spiritually nourishing.

Heresy

Now, some might argue that receiving our cues from the Spirit is not really, by strict definition, living an internal gospel, since the Holy Ghost is also an external source. This is true. Even though the Holy Ghost can reveal to us specific ways to fulfill the commandments and teach us the purpose of our obedience, a truly internal gospel would go even beyond revelation. But the point at which we begin receiving revelation is nonetheless a great turning point in our eternal progression, for revelation is the process by which light and truth become a part of us. Consider the following passages of scripture.

> Behold, that which you hear is as the voice of one crying in the wilderness—in the wilderness, because you cannot see him—my voice because *my voice is Spirit, my Spirit is truth, truth abideth and hath no end, and if it be in you it shall abound.*
>
> And if your eye be single to my glory, *your whole bodies shall be filled with light,* and there shall be no darkness in you; and that body which is filled with light comprehendeth all things (D&C 88:66-67, italics mine).

> That which is of God is light; and he that receiveth light, and continueth in God, receiveth more light; *and that light groweth brighter and brighter until the perfect day* (D&C 50:24, italics mine).

> And I, John, saw that he [Christ] received not of the fulness at the first, but received grace for grace;
>
> And he received not of the fulness at first, but continued from grace to grace, until he received a fulness; . . .

And I, John, bear record that he received a fulness of the glory of the Father;

And he received all power, both in heaven and on earth, *and the glory of the Father was with him, for he dwelt in him.* . . .

I give unto you these sayings that you may understand and know how to worship, and know what you worship, that you may come unto the Father in my name, *and in due time receive of his fulness.*

For if you keep my commandments you shall receive of his fulness, *and be glorified in me as I am in the Father*; therefore, I say unto you, you shall receive grace for grace (D&C 93:12-13, 16-17, 19-20).

Christ received a fulness of the glory of the Father. And what is the glory of the Father? Intelligence, or light and truth. And we can receive a fulness, grace for grace, and be glorified in Christ. What is grace? It is the "enabling power that allows men and women to lay hold on eternal life and exaltation after they have expended their own best efforts."[1] Grace is the divine power that enables us to become like the Father and the Son. It imparts light and truth to our souls, gradually glorifying us. And as we receive light and truth, it abounds within us, until we are filled with light and comprehend all things—until we have all intelligence.

This is the grand key. As we hearken to the Spirit, light and truth become a natural part of us, replacing darkness, and as we acquire more and more light and truth, we become like the Father. Joseph Smith said:

Here, then, is eternal life—to know the only wise and true God; and you have got to learn how to be Gods yourselves, and to be kings and priests to God, the same as all gods have done before you, namely, by going from one small degree to another, and from a small capacity to a great one; from grace to grace, from exaltation to exaltation, until you attain to the resurrection of the dead, and are able to dwell in everlasting burnings, and to sit in glory, as do those who sit enthroned in everlasting power.[2]

Just what does it mean, then, to become like God? It means that we have to learn—through the tutoring of the Holy Spirit—how to become independent of the Spirit. At first blush this sounds like heresy, but it is not. It is fully consistent with Lorenzo Snow's couplet, which declares our eternal potential. Does the Father have to be instructed by the Spirit in his actions and decisions? No. He has all truth and all light within himself. His glory is intelligence, or light and truth, of which he possesses a fulness. He is the source of light and truth. And that is our goal.

We must be careful, however, with this idea of becoming independent of the Spirit. We must not assume that this provides us an excuse to ever ignore the Spirit in this life. We partake of the divine nature through the Holy Ghost until light and truth abide in us and fill us. We grow in the Spirit until we are perfect, and that is a process that is never completed in this life. But this perspective is important, because when we understand our ultimate potential, we realize that the Spirit is not just given to guide and comfort and protect us throughout this life, but also to tutor us, to teach us how to become gods. For that is our destiny. And the Spirit is our teacher.

We must not only learn to follow the Spirit, we must understand the purpose of our obedient actions. Gaining this knowledge is critical, because God does not want us dependent on him forever. He does not want to have to tell us everything we should do. He wants us to acquire enough light and truth in this life that we can do many righteous acts of our own free will.

> For behold, it is not meet that I should command in all things; for he that is compelled in all things, the same is a sloth-ful and not a wise servant; wherefore he receiveth no reward.
>
> Verily I say, men should be anxiously engaged in a good cause, and do many things of their own free will, and bring to pass much righteousness;
>
> For the power is in them, wherein they are agents unto themselves. (D&C 58:26-28.)

As with any good parent, God wants his children to gradually become independent, and the weaning process begins as soon as we gain enough light and truth to understand his law in our hearts. When eternal principles become a part of our makeup, we will do what is right without being prompted, because it is natur-al for us to do so.

Remember Nephi, son of Helaman? The Lord promised him that "all things shall be done unto thee according to thy word, for thou shalt not ask that which is contrary to my will" (Helaman 10:5). Nephi perhaps reached the highest level of independence possible for a mortal being. He was not only in tune with the Spirit, but had also become so much like the Savior in thought and desire that he would ask only those things that were right-eous and proper. He was incapable of asking for inappropriate things, because his nature had become akin to the divine.

Why Exaltation Is Eternal

This brings us to another interesting question. Is it possible for an exalted being to turn from righteousness? Can God fall from god-hood? The answer, of course, is no. You don't become exalted until light and truth fill you, leaving no room for darkness. You don't become a god until your nature is changed to the point that you will not, cannot, turn from eternal truth. And, of course, those who have reached the state where they have all knowledge of past, present, and future (in other words, possess all truth), know perfectly the consequences of evil.

Besides, when one has obtained perfection, and has all knowledge and all power and perfect happiness, why would one want to throw it all away? That would be insanity, and exalted beings are not insane. It would be nothing less than an attempt to overthrow the order of eternity, and if this were possible, we would be completely unable to exercise faith in God. We can exercise faith in him is because he is perfect and unchangeable; he represents an eternal pattern. Satan rebelled against the order of eternity because he wanted the glory without having to pay the price. But God has already paid the price, he possesses the glory, and he would be a masochist to turn away from the perfect life he enjoys. And masochists do not become gods.

Not only is it impossible for exalted beings to turn from right-eousness, but mortals also can reach what we might call the point of no return, the point at which they have overcome all tendency toward evil and have proved to the Father that they will never fail him. They then receive promises regarding their eventual exalta-tion. They are promised eternal life. Says Joseph Smith:

> After a person has faith in Christ, repents of his sins, and is baptized for the remission of his sins and receives the Holy Ghost . . . , which is the first Comforter, then let him continue to humble himself before God, hungering and thirsting after

righteousness, and living by every word of God, and the Lord will soon say to him, Son, thou shalt be exalted. When the Lord has thoroughly proved him, and finds that the man is determined to serve Him at all hazards, then the man will find his calling and election made sure, then it will be his privilege to receive the other Comforter.[3]

This is wholly a matter of desire. If our desires are pure enough, God knows that nothing in earth or hell can persuade us to leave the path that leads toward godhood. And this is our destiny—to become like God. He has given us the higher laws to teach us how to work righteousness of our own free will. And he has given us the companionship of the Holy Ghost to tutor us in this school of the gods, to impart to us light and truth as we hearken to God's word, to change our nature so that we desire nothing but goodness and righteousness, to help us become increasingly independent in our quest for perfection.

7

Perfection and Uniformity

One valid question that I have heard expressed in various ways and that strikes at the heart of the individuality issue is this: "Isn't individuality just a function of mortal imperfection? If we reach our ultimate potential and become perfect, won't we all be exactly alike?" The worry here is one of losing identity and uniqueness, and this is a legitimate concern. In the celestial kingdom, when we are perfect, won't we all think exactly similar thoughts and say the precisely right words in any situation and do identical deeds? The answer, I argue, is an emphatic "No!"

Agency

If there were only one possible perfect response to any given situation, then God would necessarily be a being void of agency. He would have no choice but to act in a predetermined, specified manner. He would be nothing more than a puppet controlled by the strings of eternal circumstance. The false assumption here is that for any given situation, there is only one perfect response. But such is not the case.

Satan would have us believe that the path to perfection also leads to the elimination of personality and individual expression. And he uses this argument to waylay many while they are still in mortality. The only way you can express individuality, he whispers, is to rebel against restrictive commandments. Don't conform, he insists, subtly implying a synonymous relationship between conformity and obedience. And thus he plays upon our innate desire to exist separate and unique from every other living thing, and twists that desire into a fear of righteousness. "You'll lose your soul if you give it to Christ," he teaches. "Submission is self-abnegation." But this is a lie.

All we have to do is look at the world around us for evidence to the contrary. Think of people you know. I'm sure you'll come to the same conclusion I have—that the people with the most refreshing personalities are the most righteous and intelligent, and the people who are most uninterestingly uniform in thought and action are those whose lives are not in harmony with the Spirit or who wallow in sin and ignorance. There is sound reason behind this observation.

Individual Expressions of Righteousness

The commandments, as discussed earlier, can be divided into two broad categories: the higher laws and the lesser laws. The lesser laws are the ones we unfortunately give most attention to. They are the dos and don'ts (mostly don'ts) of our religion. Don't commit adultery. Don't smoke. Pay 10 percent of your earnings as tithing. Attend your meetings. Don't covet your neighbor's wife, car, house, boat, job, and so on. Don't steal. Don't lie. Don't swear. Do your home teaching or visiting teaching each month. Don't murder. These lesser laws define minimum levels of acceptable behavior. And if we keep the lesser laws, we inherit the terrestrial kingdom, along with all the other honorable men and women of the earth. If we fail to keep the lesser laws, we inherit the telestial kingdom.

The important point here is that there is basically one way to keep the lesser laws. I can not commit adultery in only one way—by not doing it. I can not smoke in only one way—by not smoking. And there is only one way I can pay 10 percent of my income. Nine percent doesn't cut it. Eleven percent, though commendable, by strict definition isn't "tithing" (since the word had its origin in the Old English *tien*, meaning "ten").

But there are higher laws under which such distinctions become meaningless. These laws are open-ended. They don't focus on minimum requirements. Instead of telling us not to commit adultery, they tell us to love our spouse with all our heart. Instead of saying, "Don't bear false witness," they require us to be "honest in all our dealings." Instead of requiring the payment of 10 percent of our income, they tell us we must consecrate everything, our all—our selves, our lives, our means, our time, and our talents—to the building of the kingdom. How many units is all? Is there one specific, perfect way to love your spouse with all your heart? Is there one correct way to apply your time and means and talents in building the kingdom? I think we would all agree that the possibilities for being perfect in living these laws are innumerable. There are infinite ways to fulfill the higher laws—infinite possible expressions of individual righteousness.

By contrast, there are few ways to break the lesser laws. How much individual expression is there in committing adultery, or in smoking, or in staying away from Church meetings? The primary expression is one of rebellion, the oldest and most self-deceptive brand of uniformity. Second only to rebellion is stupidity. Hard-core sinners are about as like each other as heads of cabbage, the reason being that sin makes them similar. Sin is the great equalizer, because it neutralizes agency and steals intelligence from us (see D&C 93:39). Once you're trapped in sin, your possibilities and your potential for individual expression fade away.

The righteous person, one who has preserved agency, on the other hand, finds open before him or her an expanding spectrum of opportunity for righteous expression. Isn't this what the Lord was saying when he stated: "It is not meet that I should command in all things; for he that is compelled in all things, the same is a slothful and not a wise servant; wherefore he receiveth no reward. Verily I say, men should be anxiously engaged in a good cause, and do many things of their own free will, and bring to pass much righteousness; for the power is in them, wherein they are agents unto themselves" (D&C 58:26-28). Obedience expands agency, partly because obedience brings increased intelligence, or light and truth, and increased intelligence opens the mind to new choices, new opportunities for further obedience.

I would guess that our Heavenly Father has infinite options open to him in his major work and purpose (bringing about our immortality and eternal life). I assume he has countless options available in his sculpting of our individual mortal tests, and one set of circumstances would achieve much the same result as another. Indeed, in one scriptural instance he even commanded Stephen Burnett and Eden Smith to "preach my gospel, whether to the north or to the south, to the east or to the west, it mattereth not, for ye cannot go amiss" (D&C 80:3). All choices in this instance were equal in the Lord's eyes. To limit us to one perfect response for every circumstance or one rigid plan for each individual's mortal probation would be to limit our creativity and even our perfection, which is likely more multifaceted than we can comprehend.

A Perfect Marriage

Take marriage, for instance. Prophets have explained that only in very rare instances are two people specifically intended, by some eternal decree, to marry each other. For the majority of us there are probably several, if not a multitude of, potential marriage partners who would be perfectly suitable for us in our quest to obtain eternal life. All sorts of marriages—everything from the attraction of complete opposites to the blending of similar temperaments— can result in a perfect union, an exalted couple. If perfection were so restrictive that everything had to be just so in order to achieve it, our decision on whom we should marry would sink most of us, because our chance of finding that one and only perfect mate would be infinitesimal. And what if someone, say the one and only person with whom I could build a perfect marriage, decided to live a life of sin? I'd have to settle for second best, or third or fourth, and I'd never make the grade. The only way such a universe could work would be for God to arrange all the marriages, or at least the circumstances that would result in all the right marriages. That, again, would be deterministic. God would have to infringe upon our agency to ensure that someone else's choice wouldn't adversely affect my salvation. But no one else's choices can prevent me from attaining exaltation. Only my choices affect my destiny. Obviously, the notion of one perfect action in any given situation is absolutely illogical. Perfection, in all its manifestations, must be as variable as personality.

Opposition

The issue of opposition that Lehi explained to his son Jacob is again relevant in answering the question of uniform perfection. If all exalted beings were identical, there would be no existence, for there would be no differences. The very fact that our God exists at all tells us that he is different from others of his high standing. He and other exalted beings are not a "compound in one." He is our Father in Heaven.

And we have a Mother in Heaven who stands in a special opposition to our eternal Father. These two together, however, are not mere three-dimensional photocopies of some eternally repetitious personality pattern. In fact, if all gods were exactly the same in what they would think, do, and say in any given situation, the universe would be a horribly lonely and monotonous place, for communicating with anyone else would be like talking to yourself, and watching other exalted beings do anything would be like looking in the mirror. I would suppose that the myriad worlds created by the gods throughout the universe are as diverse in their construction as the gods are different from each other.

Hugh Nibley has pointed out that creativity is a frontier activity, always. By definition it has to be. If we "create" something that has been done before, we have not really created it. "What is creation?" Nibley asks. "An endless procession of worlds rolling off the assembly line? No, creation never duplicates; it is never mere production after a set mold. Creation begins where everything else, everything that has been done so far, has reached its utmost limit of accomplishment."[1] God lives a life of endless, supremely individual, creative expression.

Variety, the fact that others are different from us and create things that are different from our creations, gives us a background against which we can define ourselves. We can only know ourselves to the extent that we differ from others. And mimicking others makes us less unique and actually robs us of certain aspects of our personalities. Hence, those who feel comparatively inferior and attempt to copy those whose personalities they envy are really making themselves less significant, not more.

When I was younger, I had a good friend who possessed a very likeable and dominant personality. I admired him, as did everyone else who knew him, and, perhaps unthinkingly, I began to imitate him. After a while I became aware of what I was doing. Especially in his presence I found myself doing things I thought he would approve of and saying things I thought he would say. I felt my own individuality becoming less, as if it was being swallowed up in the glow of his (as I perceived it) more radiant personality. My unique identity was vanishing. I began to see myself as a weak reflection of his mannerisms, attitudes, and values—not that they were in any way bad, but they just weren't *me*. Naturally, the feeling was very discomforting, because I was not being who I really should have been and, as a consequence, began to lose sight of my own identity. Fortunately, I became aware of what was happening and was able to step back and reevaluate my actions, recapture the independence I had begun to give away.

Perfectionism

Perfectionism is a great stifler of personality, indeed a great hindrance to achieving perfection. Webster's defines perfectionism as "a disposition to regard anything short of perfection as unacceptable." Perfectionists castigate themselves for their failings and are unforgiving toward themselves. By contrast, it is a sign of spiritual maturity when individuals can recognize that we mortals often learn by our mistakes and that if we are moving forward, there is no reason to condemn ourselves.

Our Eternal Father is not so hard on us. He does not condemn us when we try and fail, and he gladly extends forgiveness when we get up, brush ourselves off, and try to do better next time. He understands that perfection is not an off-the-rack suit of clothes that we can simply acquire in a minute and put on at will. It is a very individual, step-by-step process that will take us this whole life and an unrevealed portion of the next to create.

Perfectionism, we might say, is just another name for self-rejection, because we are all imperfect. When we are perfectionists, we have in our heads some illusory notion of perfection that is inevitably the product of either external expectations or our own misperceptions of those around us. We see others in the false light of envy, blind to their warts and blemishes, perceiving only their superiority to our own meager qualities. We translate that perception into an incredibly demanding, self-demeaning pursuit of excellence. We expect of ourselves a perfection created by our misperception of others. And so we put ourselves down because we have built up illusions to veil the imperfections of our fellow mortals.

Perfectionism, if anything, is a denial of our own uniqueness. By definition, it is an unrealistic view of ourselves. We are not perfect. Neither is anyone else. We should not see them as such. Of course we should not become critical and cynical about others, but we should recognize that they have strengths and weaknesses within the context of their individual personalities just as we do. We can learn from the good qualities of others, but we should never hate ourselves because of their goodness.

Our own perfection will be different from everyone else's, and when we begin filling in the missing gaps in our personalities and realizing an expansion of our own unique qualities, we will feel an incredible sense of wholeness, even though we may realize that we're not yet perfect. The joy of discovering the correct pattern for our unique personality and seeing it take shape is much like the wonder of seeing a beautiful picture emerge from the myriad separate pieces of an intricate jigsaw puzzle. We can recognize much of the picture long before it is completely assembled—enough of it, in fact, to understand that in its complete and correct form it will have a uniqueness and beauty of its own. And we will also see that any stray pieces from other pictures (that may perchance have found their way into our puzzle box) will look out of place and detract from the beautiful image we are assembling.

Each child of God is unique, and that uniqueness is not just a function of our weaknesses. It is not something that will vanish when we become perfect. As we overcome our weaknesses and express ourselves more fully in righteousness, our individuality is enhanced and perfected. This is not to say, however, that we should become self-absorbed in trying to be different from others, just for the sake of being unique. Indeed, in many ways we should be like others. Just because the majority of Church members believes abortion to be wrong does not give us a valid excuse for taking the opposing view. Perfection lies in finding out who we really are, what our own unique talents and strengths and personality are, and striving to magnify them. And the fact that we can learn many things about our eternal destiny only through divine revelation supports the doctrine that perfection comes not through effort alone, but through Christ.

8

Self

<figure>Decorative divider</figure>

Our modern society is extremely self-conscious. We are preoccupied with self. We have psychoanalysts and self-help groups; we worry about our self-esteem and self-confidence; and we have witnessed a whole generation trying to get in touch with itself. Self is both a popular magazine and a prefix that fills three pages of my dictionary with self-words, from *self-abasement* to *self-worth*. So how should we regard self? And how should we regard our preoccupation with self? Is it good or bad? Is it self-centered for a person to seek to know him- or herself? Should we consciously seek to have self-esteem, or should we just forget about self?

Two Extremes

Since opposition seems to be a major theme of this book, let's look at two oppositional views of self that we sometimes find among Latter-day Saints. On the one hand we have a multitude of members who are perhaps excessively concerned with self-esteem—their own and everyone else's. "I don't like myself," is the existential cry of souls in our troubled generation. "I'm too short, too fat, too tall, too thin, too ugly, too beautiful (no one appreciates my personality), too shy, too overbearing, too dumb, too smart (no one understands me), too klutzy, too athletic (everyone's jealous), too obnoxious, too boring, too insecure, too arrogant, too human." Hence, the plethora of books that preach the pseudo-doctrine of self-esteem and encourage us to incessantly take our temperature to see if we are happy, confident, and likeable.

These self-consumed individuals bend the scriptures just enough to convince themselves that narcissism is not only healthy, but is actually a commandment. "Thou shalt love thy neighbor as thyself" (Matthew 19:19) gets twisted around to mean "Thou shalt love thyself, and thy neighbor too." Even in our service to others, our first obligation is to self. "If you would lift another, you must stand on higher ground" is this group's favorite maxim.

Another group, however, holds an exactly opposite view and suggests that we should totally ignore self. "He that findeth his life shall lose it: and he that loseth his life for my sake shall find it" (Matthew 10:39) is this group's favorite scripture. (Translation: If you forget yourself and serve others, you will find yourself.) These selfless souls have adopted two popular platitudes as their slogans. The first is a catchy little verse that goes something like this:

I sought myself, myself I could not see;
I sought my God, my God eluded me;
I sought my brother and found all three.

The second is: "Help your brother's boat across, and lo, yours has reached the other shore," or something to that effect. The idea is easy to comprehend. If you focus totally on your neighbor, you will automatically become perfect.

These two views, I believe, are not only extreme, they are also simplistic and even spiritually dangerous. The first can lead to constricting blindness, the inability to see the needs of anyone other than self. When we elevate self-love to the status of divine edict, we can become distractedly egocentric as well as either self-righteous or self-condemning. The overwhelming scope of my needs, my opinions, my weaknesses, my problems, my successes effectively paralyzes me and prevents me from doing anyone any good. Note that the Lord did not command us to love ourselves. He simply took for granted that we already do. And rightly so. Even those who are critical of themselves, who claim to have low self-esteem and to not like themselves, actually love themselves desperately. If they didn't love themselves, they wouldn't be so concerned about their performance or their feelings of inadequacy. The fact that they are concerned proves that they care deeply about their lives—regardless of how much self-flagellation they mete out. Elder Jeffrey R. Holland once spoke of the dangers of this first perspective:

> The threat I fear . . . is the threat of self-centeredness gone amuck, of psychic insistence upon everyone doing his own thing, of everyone getting in touch with himself at the expense of getting in touch with anyone else. It is the threat of a culture which has in some ways carried accentuated individualism to the extreme and now has the pursuit of happiness standing paralyzed in front of a mirror, pleading, "Mirror, mirror on the wall, who's the fairest of them all?" . . .

> In a world where it is all hanging out, where we have immersed ourselves in ourselves, . . . we run the risk, in our quest for instant gratification and purely personal views of our world, of profoundly violating the two great commandments on which all others depend. We may come to find neither love of God nor love of neighbor, but only love of ourselves. Should that ever be so, then, as Pogo Possum would say: "We have met the enemy, and he is us."[1]

The second view, that we should simply ignore self, has equally perilous consequences. Much has been said about the "unexamined life," and rightly so. We have been counseled to keep journals, not only because they forge links between generations, but also because journal writing helps us examine our lives, learn the lessons we came to mortality to learn, and express feelings we wouldn't (and shouldn't) dare expose to anyone else.

Ignoring self is as spiritually unhealthy as being totally self-absorbed. Those who are so busy helping their brother's boat across, may not even notice that their own boat has gaping holes in it. I recall a situation that occurred in my mission. We had just welcomed a new mission president, and he was rather unique in his ability to motivate people. Throughout the mission elders and sisters were working longer hours—willingly, eagerly. Baptisms increased, as did the spirit in the mission. But two zone leaders misunderstood the message and neglected the balance that is needed even in the Lord's work. They would leave their apartment early each morning and return home late in the evening. They also weren't taking the customary preparation day. Their hours may have been impressive, but they were leaving themselves inadequate time for such things as scripture study, prayer, and meditation. When the mission president caught wind of this, he immediately told them to stop it and set them back on course, telling them they were committing spiritual suicide.

Between the Two Extremes

There has to be a balance. Overzealous service won't compensate for ignorance. And endless self-improvement does not excuse us from paying attention to our neighbors. I can't explain this balance, as I perceive it, without referring to an experience I had when I was a university student.

This experience, I suppose, could be called an identity crisis, not an uncommon ordeal. For one reason or another, I was struggling. I felt that my life was fragmented, that it was running in several directions at the same time. And I wasn't pleased with how I was performing in most of these disparate arenas. I came face to face with the most basic question of life: Who am I? Well, at that point I didn't really know. I was no longer Elder Terry. That much was certain. Elder Terry had mysteriously vanished somewhere over the Atlantic, and when the plane had touched down on American soil, I was just plain old Roger Terry. And yet I was not the same Roger Terry who had left for Germany two years before. That young man had been overly influenced by sports, peers, appearances, and teenage myopia. He wouldn't have been able to either verbalize his philosophy of life or give an inventory of his strengths, weaknesses, and interests.

Elder Terry, on the other hand, could have told you that tracting developed character (and even uncovered a few investigators if you knew how to do it right), that he loved the German people, and that he was a hard worker who sincerely tried not to aspire to leadership positions (even though he secretly believed that he deserved them). He could also have added that, by and large, he was happy and busy and had a strong testimony. But had he been around when the postmission crisis hit, he couldn't have told me what to major in or even why I should be at the university in the first place. He couldn't have given me any useful advice on dating and couldn't have explained why I felt so spiritually out of sorts, even though I was getting up every morning at 5:30 to read the scriptures. Perhaps that's why he bailed out over the Atlantic. He knew he didn't belong in my shoes. And my shoes were feeling pretty uncomfortable to me during that adjustment period.

I floundered for a while. And then I did something that is perhaps the most intelligent and inspired thing I've ever done. I didn't try to get in touch with myself or worry myself sick over my unhappiness and perceived low self-esteem. I didn't seek counseling or join any self-help groups. And I didn't "seek my brother" and immerse myself in his problems as an escape from (or cure for) my own difficulties. I simply turned to the one person in the universe who absolutely, perfectly understood me. I sought God. I found a place where I could be alone, and over the course of several months I spent dozens of hours on my knees. I didn't plead for self-knowledge. I pled for spiritual strength, for a feeling of nearness to my Father. And it was hard work. But the hours spent were richly rewarded. At length I felt the veil part ever so slightly, and a holy influence entered my heart.

This experience taught me some vital lessons. I learned, for instance, that the only real cure for what we call low self-esteem is faith in Christ. When you are encompassed by the spirit and feel a nearness to God's love, you cannot feel anything but infinite worth. The problems and perplexities of life then fit into a larger, more sensible context, and you recognize that with God's help you can handle just about anything. This, I suppose, is a fairly good definition of faith.

Through this communion I also learned about myself, my real self. During those moments when the veil was parted, I was shown brief glimpses of my eternal identity, my potential. I came to understand that separate from my temporal problems and circumstances is something incredibly permanent and eternal, like an anchor in the innermost chambers of my soul, something that has had an eternity of experience and development and yet is not complete. I was shown only glimpses—and those glimpses were sketchy. They revealed something you might call a spiritual outline or silhouette, something seen "through a glass darkly." But I saw enough to recognize that I am a unique individual, that I have an eternal personality that seeks to be liberated from some of the chains I have bound it with here on earth. I also saw that this personality has a unique destiny, a potential which it has not yet achieved. During these moments of communion I would see myself, almost in vision, acting in certain ways that felt so utterly genuine to me that I longed to be the person I saw, for the gap between what I was and what I could become was real and significant. Nonetheless, I could envision my potential, my destiny, and I knew how right it was for me.

But the real lesson in all this is that when I was shown the person I could and should become, I always saw that person interacting with others. The message was impossible to misunderstand. My perfect eternal identity was an individual who would treat people in a particular way, would feel certain feelings about them, would talk in a distinct manner to them—and it all felt so real and natural and right. I was being shown who I was supposed to become, and this eternal identity, I discovered, exists in and is defined by relationships with others.

I learned that there is a perfect pattern for me, and that if I make certain choices, I can eventually fulfill that perfection. A balance, however, is absolutely essential. I am not to single-mindedly seek my own individual fulfillment to the exclusion of everyone else's needs (a real temptation). My eventual perfection is dependent upon relationships with others. The Lord's commandments insist upon this. Likewise, I am not to ignore the question of what I can become and simply direct my undivided attention toward the problems and perplexities of others. Everything I do in relationships is to be done with an eye on that perfect pattern I have seen. And, of course, everything is to be done with an eye single to the glory of God, for he is our master, our tutor, our Father, and, at present, our only completely intimate friend.

Aloneness vs. Alienation

Mortality, as we have discussed, comes with limits and boundaries. Our view, not only of ourselves and our eternal potential, but also of everything around us, is remarkably hazy. We do "see through a glass darkly" (1 Cor. 13:12). In an earlier chapter we discussed the idea that we see the world around us, past and present, in a very incomplete manner. The future we don't see at all. Each person has a limited and imperfect perspective on truth and reality. Our communication with others is also extremely limited. Try as I might, I cannot really make someone else understand anything I have experienced. I can talk about my life, my feelings, my perspective, but words are incredibly inadequate tools of expression.

The ultimate frustration in mortality is to come face to face with the fact that no one truly understands us. We all want to be understood—some of us desperately—but even in the best of marriage relationships, communication and understanding are never perfect. Let me illustrate. One day not so long ago my family and I returned home from visiting my wife's parents. It was a late summer evening, and it was raining gently. We put the children to bed, then my wife busied herself with some project or other while I went out and sat on the front steps and smelled the rain. It was a singular experience. Can I describe the scent of summer rain? Perhaps, but I won't try. Can I explain the feelings that fragrance evoked in me? Not in the least. And I thought about that for a moment as I sat on the steps. I didn't talk to my wife about that experience. I suspect she doesn't feel the same way about summer rain as I do. I know for a fact that she could never, at least in mortality, understand the wonderful feelings and memories that came to me on that breath of rainwashed summer air. Those feelings are mine, not hers.

The experiences of mortality are ours to savor, but not ours to share. Not yet. Only God understands us completely. Only he can feel what we feel, see through our eyes, as it were. As mentioned earlier, were this not the case, he would be unfit to judge us. This is one of the great and bittersweet burdens of mortality. We so deeply long to share our most poignant joys, our most exquisite disappointments. We long to be understood by our fellow mortals. But the necessities of mortality preclude that blessing.

We are alone in this earth life—unless we can find our way back into the presence of that one individual who can and does understand us fully. And perhaps there is purpose in this arrangement, for no possession, no experience, no object, and no individual should be more important to us than he is. This must be so, otherwise we would not be fit to return to his presence, where we will have restored to us the ability to communicate at a more intimate and meaningful level—where we will know even as we are known (see I Cor. 13:12). Perhaps this is one reason why, in terms of our relationships with other mortals, we are alone. But just because we are alone doesn't mean that we must be alienated from each other.

There is a difference between aloneness and alienation. The difference lies in how we deal with our restricted mortal perspective and our limited ability to communicate. If we fail to understand the fact that we don't really see the world correctly, that our perspective is flawed by its narrowness, then we generally treat our fellowmen in one of two ways. We either judge and condemn them because they don't live according to the criteria we have set up (in our minds) as correct, or we try to persuade them to accept our way of seeing life, try to force them to change—their mind, their behavior, their identity. We can classify either manifestation of this fundamental blindness as dogmatism, which is defined as: (1) positiveness in assertion of opinion, especially when unwarranted or arrogant, and (2) a viewpoint or system of ideas based on insufficiently examined premises. And either of these forms of dogmatism alienates us from our fellow mortals, because no one wants to hear: "I'm right and you're wrong." Chances are, in most situations in life, both sides are a little bit wrong and a little bit right.

But even when God has revealed that my view is more or less correct and someone else's is flawed, my inability to communicate can cause real problems and alienate others. An experience I had in the mission field will illustrate. One spring afternoon my senior companion and I found a man we were sure was "golden." He was a strong personality, a leader in the community. We taught him about Joseph Smith and the Restoration, and he agreed with everything we said. We were so impressed by him that we started referring to him between ourselves as Bishop Geerdts. He went on vacation for several weeks after our first discussion, and we anxiously awaited our second meeting. Before he returned, however, my companion was transferred and I received a new partner fresh from the MTC. "Bishop Geerdts" eventually returned, we set an appointment, and a few days later pedaled our bikes out to his home for our second discussion.

We intended to teach him about the plan of salvation, but Herr Geerdts (no longer "Bishop") had other ideas. In fact, he had his own ideas about everything—the purpose of life, the pre-existence, the resurrection—and he was not about to let some twenty-year-old kid teach him about the gospel. He had his opinions, and he felt they were every bit as valid as mine. He had thought them out, and they made perfect sense to him. Now, I had a testimony about the things I was teaching. I knew through personal revelation that I was right and he was wrong. And apparently that message came through loud and clear. But do you think I could make him understand what I knew to be true? There are not words in any mortal language—especially not in English or German, both of which he spoke fluently—to communicate those things to him. Oh, he understood well enough the doctrines I was trying to convince him of, but he didn't believe they were true. To him, his views were correct.

The discussion that night, I am ashamed to admit, became rather intense, for neither side was willing to budge. And at that point the Lord took charge. A power came over me, and words came from my mouth that I had never intended, words that would have never occurred to me that night because of my frustration: "If you'll pray about the things we've told you tonight," I heard my voice say, "God will reveal the truth to you." That was it. I knew—I had an immediate witness—that those words were true. But I also received an assurance that he would not pray about it. He never did.

The lesson I learned from this experience is both sobering and significant. Even when we are right and know that we are right, we cannot convince others of the truth. They will always have the free agency to refuse to believe us. We can alienate them, of course, by forcing our views on them, even when our views are inspired, but we cannot communicate directly to their spirits the things we know and have experienced. Only God can communicate the truth in a manner that leaves no doubt. And the Spirit can communicate truth *through* us at times. But independently, we are not allowed to influence others in that manner. We are separate from each other.

And this, I suppose, is the lesson. Because we are so disconnected from others by the constraints of mortality, because our perspective is so limited, and because we have such difficulties communicating with and understanding each other, we must make a conscious effort to accommodate these barriers. We can't simply judge others by our narrow view of reality. Only God can judge them, for only he understands their experiences, their feelings, their intentions, their weaknesses. Unless inspired to do so, we also cannot insist that our particular viewpoint is the only correct one. That not only alienates people, but often embarrasses us in the long run.

Likewise, we can't demand that others change, even if we are certain they are wrong. We often violate the agency of others even in preaching repentance. Read Section 121 of the Doctrine & Covenants carefully, and you'll realize that only the Spirit, speaking at times through us, can command a person to repent. On our own, we can show a better way by example, we can teach correct principles, we can even offer our views for others to think about and discuss with us, but we can't insist that someone repent. That, says the Lord, is exercising "control . . . or compulsion upon the souls of the children of men, in . . . unrighteousness" (D&C 121:37). Repentance must come from within—within an individual's agency, as prompted by the Spirit. Hyrum Smith was given some valuable counsel by the Lord. He was commanded: "Say nothing but repentance unto this generation" (D&C 11:9). But the Lord qualified that commandment later in the same revelation: "Seek not to declare my word, but first seek to obtain my word, and then shall your tongue be loosed; then, if you desire, you shall have my Spirit and my word, yea, *the power of God unto the convincing of men*" (verse 21, italics mine).

By the same token, we shouldn't always talk and never listen, because that also alienates us from others and prevents us from accepting the notion that other people have just as much right to their perspectives as we do to ours. And we mustn't be careless in our attempts at communication. Language is so imprecise and our ability to comprehend other people's intentions and motives is so utterly meager that we should take special care to not send ambiguous messages to others and not draw erroneous assumptions from the inevitably inadequate messages others send to us. Communication requires a healthy dose of tolerance, patience, silent listening, acceptance, and gentle encouragement. Our best attempts at communication are more an equal and gentle clasping of hands than a board to hit people over the head with.

Communication, in general, is an attempt to make our aloneness bearable, and as such it requires a healthy regard for self—on both sides. I must be myself and remain true to the sense of identity I feel within, while allowing others the same privilege. If I am constantly changing my own viewpoint or even my personality to fit what I perceive as the other person's Weltanschauung, then I am both less genuine and less interesting than I should be, for it is our differences that make us refreshing to each other. I may admire another individual's personality, but if I mimic it, I have become as interesting to that person as a conversation with the mirror. It is our diversity that makes us attractive to each other. Where everyone is merely trying to impress everyone else, no one develops long-term, meaningful relationships.

The Soul's Mirror

Are you comfortable with yourself? That can be an uncomfortable question. I read a few years ago about a study that asked a group of professors at Stanford University "to sit still in a room for twenty-five minutes—without reading, listening to music, or talking to anyone—several gave up before the allotted time had passed."[2] "Many Americans find themselves simply unable to unwind" the article stated. Have we developed a habit of being so distracted with the busyness of life that to sit alone with our thoughts and feelings has become an uncomfortable experience?

Contrast this with the forty-five minutes I spent on my steps smelling and listening to the summer shower. Many things crossed my mind that evening as I sat and enjoyed the rain. But I wasn't communing with myself, and I wasn't communing with nature. I was simply experiencing something enjoyable, and though it brought to mind many wonderful memories, the experience was completely present-tense. I was experiencing life. I was feeling something significant. And I didn't feel any need to talk about it. I knew I couldn't explain it to my wife. When she poked her head out the door and looked at me, wondering what on earth I was doing, I just smiled. I was completely comfortable with my own silent savoring of life.

Nature, someone once observed, is the true mirror of the soul. I believe this. As I listened to the summer rain, smelled its dusty fragrance, and listened to its gentle rhythm, I saw my reflection in it. It brought out the best of my feelings and my uniquely personal sensitivities. And I reveled in the experience. Nature is a reservoir of passion. It is God's immediate creation.

As a boy, growing up in the hills and fields north of Ogden, Utah, I was in touch with God's creation. I can still remember parting the blades of grass to see what was going on down deep, near the soil. I climbed trees, hiked hills and mountains, dipped my bare feet in icy streams, irrigated my grandfather's orchards, explored ant hills, caught snakes, and played in the rain. The world was a wide and wonderful place, filled with surprises and joys and discoveries, and my identity was somehow bound up with all those experiences. When I grew up and left my boyhood home as a missionary to faraway Germany, an absolutely beautiful land, I was still constantly out in the elements. I mostly rode a bicycle or walked. The wind and rain and sunshine were my daily companions. The salt on the North Sea breeze, the fragrance of flowers, the texture of tree bark, the warmth of the May sunshine, the sound of autumn leaves rustling in the wind, the grey-green hue of twilight in September—these things touched places in my soul and taught me things about myself. I was in tune with the world around me, and it was a mirror in which I could view my soul. By contrast, it has occurred to me rather often of late that my life is so much less full now that I ride in a closed automobile, separate from my surroundings, sit behind a desk complete with artificial wood veneer, and stare at an aesthetically neutral computer screen five days a week. Perhaps that is why the summer rain meant so much. Perhaps that is why I also enjoy working in the garden. It brings me back to who I really am.

Our world is becoming a passionless world. And as people become more self-centered, they also, ironically, become more selfless. When I say selfless, I don't mean unselfish, but rather that people have *less self*, that they are losing a vital portion of themselves. When we find ourselves staring constantly at sterile walls and artificial-silk plants in antiseptically clean and functional corporate offices, our environment still is our mirror, and we see ourselves reflected in it. In such an environment, self is diminished, and with it the differences between people. And when self is diminished, we communicate on a functional level, for anything truly interesting and life-giving seems foreign and out-of-place in such a barren setting. Something of life, one might say, is lost. This is a great tragedy for individuals in modern society.

9

Relationships

One well-documented consequence of the rise of large, impersonal organizations in 20th-century America is the alienation of individuals from each other. This is caused by the common practice of viewing people as tools of the organizations in which they work. Organizational vernacular is even rather open and unapologetic about this. Businesses frequently refer to individuals as "assets" or "human resources" or "human capital." These terms imply that people are employed to serve the needs of the organization, not the other way around. Says Neil W. Chamberlain:

> Employees are being paid to produce, not to make themselves into better people. Corporations are purchasing employee time to make a return on it, not investing in employees to enrich their lives. Employees are human capital, and when capital is hired or leased the objective is not to embellish it for its own

sake but to use it for financial advantage. But somewhere in this philosophy there is an inconsistency with the notion of a society of self-governing individuals. The large corporation has become an organizer of people, a user of people, a molder of identities, according to criteria that it has evolved, without regard to the effect on those people except as this is registered on the balance sheet.[1]

This, some might say, is merely good business. To organize in any other way would be economically impractical. "The idea that organizations should be built up round and adjusted to individual idiosyncrasies," says Lyndall Urwick, "rather than that individuals should be adapted to the requirements of sound principles of organization, is as foolish as attempting to design an engine to accord with the whimsies of one's maiden aunt rather than with the laws of mechanical science."[2]

This view notwithstanding, many secular institutions today are pursuing a sort of organizational revolution, recognizing the fundamental rights and needs of their employees. Most institutions, however, still adhere to the traditional position that people are resources, tools to be used in gaining financial advantage. When this philosophy persists in an organization, people become alienated from each other. Why? Because, as David K. Hart points out, "if one must consider oneself as a function, then one must also consider others as functions. . . . [I]n modern organizations, individuals are linked to other individuals in artificial relationships defined solely by the organizational mission."[3] It is not friendship, but a person's function within the organization that determines his or her associations.

What, you might well ask, does all this have to do with the topics discussed in this book? Well, it is not my purpose here to try to reform all the economic and government bureaucracies in America. I merely wish to point out that many others have been concerned about this phenomenon, and that we Latter-day Saints are not at all unaffected by our contact with the world and its organizations.

Functional Relationships

Most modern organizations, as mentioned above, treat people as functions, and, generally speaking, those functions are fairly specific. Corporations have accountants, marketing directors, clerks, product managers, foremen, financial vice-presidents, computer programmers, quality inspectors, secretaries, assembly workers, machinists, researchers, and inventory controllers. Each person has a function, a specialization, and interacts with others in his or her specialization. If a person associates with someone outside that function, the resulting relationship is usually dictated by cross-functional exchange and remains, nonetheless, a functional relationship.

Generally, these organizational relationships are narrow, superficial, and impersonal. They are, to use an acceptable current euphemism, "professional relationships," and sometimes we become so adept at that type of interaction with people that we find it spilling over into all our relationships, even among neighbors and fellow ward members. But the LDS ward, in its ideal form, is a community of saints. And a community is the exact opposite of the specialized, organizational relationships we learn in corporations and other institutional bureaucracies. In a community, individuals are indispensable to each other, friendships have depth, and communication is neither functional nor superficial. The key words here are friendship and communication—two essential elements in any community. Two stories will perhaps illustrate what I am trying to say.

A couple of years ago, we had living in our Orem, Utah, ward a young nonmember family from Ohio. The husband and wife were fine people, devoted to their family and their Catholic religion. They should have fit in very well in the neighborhood. The wife—let's call her Tammy—even asked to be a visiting teacher, so that her Mormon neighbors could get to know her and see that she was willing to reach out to them. She did this with no intention of ever joining the Church.

Tammy happened to report her visiting teaching to my wife, and they became fairly good friends. I knew Tammy's husband—let's call him Bob—because we both played on the ward basketball team. Bob and Tammy were not the martyr type. They were outgoing, and they invited us to parties at their home, which we gladly attended along with several of our LDS neighbors. Bob and Tammy had no interest in joining the Church, but that didn't stop them from making the best of their situation. They were trying to be good neighbors and develop close friendships, but they were growing increasingly frustrated.

One day when Tammy was reporting her visiting teaching, she confided to my wife that she and Bob felt ostracized. When Sheri asked why, Tammy explained that it was because they had no close friends in the neighborhood. "Whenever the women get together," she said, "all they talk about is Primary." They found that their LDS neighbors were too busy to develop the close friendships she and Bob were accustomed to. She assumed they felt ostracized because they didn't attend our church and that the Mormon Church provided the major bond between its members.

But as Sheri and I talked about this, we were somewhat startled to conclude that we felt exactly as our Catholic neighbors did. We had lived in the area for two years, and though we had many casual friends, we hadn't developed any close, enduring friendships. "There's not a sister in the ward I feel comfortable calling on the phone, just to chat," is the way Sheri described it. She felt comfortable calling other sisters only if she had a reason to—a function-to-function type relationship. My experience was similar. I played basketball with a fairly large group of men in the ward every Wednesday night and was on amicable terms with more than half the ward, but I didn't have any close friends either. All my communication was either in the context of basketball or work or church assignments.

After talking about it, we decided we'd fallen unwittingly into an all-too-common pattern. We related to people on a friendly, functional, superficial level, but were not part of a community, not in the best sense of the word. Granted, we had lived in the area for only a couple of years, and things gradually changed, but at the time we didn't have the kind of meaningful relationships we enjoyed with, say, mission companions or childhood friends. And that brings me to my second story.

When I was a teenager, growing up in North Ogden, Utah, our house was on the edge of civilization (as I knew it). Across the street was a long stretch of scrub oak that ran almost unbroken to the base of Ben Lomond, the majestic mountain that stands at the head of the Salt Lake Valley. At the foot of Ben Lomond is Willow Springs, a popular camping spot in those days for backpackers and hikers. Sometimes in the summer, a few friends and I would pack some food and sleeping bags, hike the few miles up to Willow Springs, and camp out under the stars and the oaks and the maples (ironically, there weren't any willows).

After the campfire had burned down to a bed of glowing embers, we would retire to our sleeping bags, gaze up at the sprawling splendor of the Milky Way and talk about important things. We were young teenagers, and as full of hormones and hero worship as the next guy, but we didn't talk about girls or baseball (which were usually on our minds). We talked in awed tones about the mysteries of eternity. We pondered aloud childish questions such as: "If God has a father, and he has a father, and he has a father, where did it all begin? It had to start somewhere." We talked about infinite space. And we swapped our meager knowledge, dredged up from forgotten sources, about the universe and astronomy, and tried to put a few pieces of the eternal puzzle together. We may not have actually spoken the question, but it was there, lurking in the shadows of our moonlit conversations: "Who am I—and where in all this vastness of time and space do I fit in?"

The reason I bring this up is not because we felt we were unusual. I don't think we were. I bring it up simply because it is one of the most precious memories I have of my youth. To put this in perspective, I don't remember a single Aaronic Priesthood lesson or sacrament meeting talk. But I remember sleeping out under the stars with my friends and talking about what were, to us, significant ideas. These were the deepest, most profound thoughts our teenage minds could conjure up. And we shared them. We were friends, in the truest sense.

I don't talk about profound ideas with my friends now. I ask how their work is going, or how their sick child is, or how to install a sprinkling system, or how to tighten a belt on the car air conditioner. Even when I teach the Gospel Doctrine class in my ward, I fail to achieve the meaningful exchange I'm talking about. Because of the requirement to cover a certain amount of outlined material, most—but not all—of my communication in class is rather formal and functional.

Maybe that's why I'm writing this book. We need to start a dialogue in the Church somehow, a dialogue that we adults cannot afford to let youthful campers have a monopoly on, a dialogue that touches the ideas that stir men's souls. Perhaps this is my attempt to jump-start a neglected engine. Perhaps we're just too busy, now that we're adults, to take time to think—and talk—about eternity and put our lives in that context. Especially lacking in this meaningful type of communication are our endless planning and leadership meetings—from ward councils to high councils. I wonder at times if we will be held accountable for wasting each other's time in the way we administer the Lord's work. "How vain and trifling have been our spirits, our conferences, our councils, our meetings, our private as well as public conversations," wrote Joseph Smith from Liberty Jail, "too low, too mean, too vulgar, too condescending for the dignified characters of the called and chosen of God."[4] This, I gather, is not a new problem.

Community

The preceding chapters have focused on the individual, because the individual is the focal point of the gospel. We are responsible for our own sins, not someone else's; we must contend with our own weaknesses and build our own strengths; we must work out our own salvation. These are individual tasks—no one else can do them for us. But we are not alone in the world. We belong to a community of saints. And we will not be alone in the eternities. In a sense, we will be wonderfully and perfectly "together" there, because of how we will be able to communicate.

Our community of saints here on earth is now more than nine million in number and growing rapidly. It is an organization more vast and complex than the largest multinational corporation. The challenges of holding it together, and holding it on course, are monumental. Because of this, we must make a conscious effort to keep the community aspects of the Church alive and to remember that we are not tools of the organization, mere functions in a great organizational mission. We serve *in* the Church, but we do not serve the Church. We serve each other, and we serve the Lord. The Church is merely a vehicle through which the Lord helps individuals gain salvation and reach their eternal potential.

It would perhaps be wise for us to remember that the Church is temporary in nature. It has not always existed on earth—the Lord has used several types of organization throughout history to fulfill his purposes—and it will not exist in the eternities. There, a different, more permanent organization abides. There is indeed order in eternity, but that order is always subordinate to and exists to serve individuals, not the reverse. God's work and glory is to "bring to pass the immortality and eternal life of man" (Moses 1:39), not of any particular organization. And he chooses his tools wisely.

10

Expanding the Mortal Mind

Several years ago I was writing a book on leadership for a consulting group. Their work took them to organizations across the country where they helped business executives improve their leadership skills. They expressed concern over a phenomenon they saw everywhere they went: adult Americans, by and large, have stopped learning. It's a cultural thing, they explained. Learning is something for kids. When you become an adult, you are supposed to have all the answers. This attitude complicated their work, for improvement implies change, and change comes only through learning. Their biggest challenge was getting adults to accept the fact that they don't know everything, that they must continue learning and changing—indefinitely.

This same principle applies to us as Latter-day Saints. "A man is saved," says the Prophet, "no faster than he gets knowledge." Why? Because "if he does not get knowledge, he will be brought into captivity by some evil power in the other world, as evil spirits will have more knowledge, and consequently more power than many men who are on the earth."[1]

Our theology insists on continual improvement, constant learning. But what kind of learning? "Knowledge of the things of God," says Joseph. This is most important. But we aren't to limit our study to the scriptures or *The Ensign* or "church books." "And as all have not faith, seek ye diligently and teach one another words of wisdom," says the Lord, "yea, seek ye out of the best books words of wisdom; seek learning, even by study and also by faith" (D&C 88:118). "Study and learn, and become acquainted with all good books, and with languages, tongues, and people" (D&C 90:15). Inherent in this commandment is the notion that we must first be able to distinguish a good book from a poor one.

We are to learn "of things both in heaven and in the earth, and under the earth; things which have been, things which are, things which must shortly come to pass; things which are at home, things which are abroad; the wars and perplexities of the nations, and the judgments which are upon the land; and a knowledge also of countries and of kingdoms" (D&C 88:79). An expanding knowledge of the world we live in as well as the world that is our eternal home is part of our religion. Why? Because knowledge is power, and the more knowledge we have, the greater our chances will be of gaining exaltation.

"The things of God are of deep import; and time, and experience, and careful and ponderous and solemn thoughts can only find them out. Thy mind, O man! if thou wilt lead a soul unto salvation, must stretch as high as the utmost heavens, and search into and contemplate the darkest abyss, and the broad expanse of eternity—thou must commune with God."[2] This notion of adult learning, of expanding the mortal mind throughout our lives, is a serious matter with the Lord and his prophets.

Sequential Learning

Elder John A. Widtsoe taught that the only knowledge that will help us in establishing a satisfactory religion is true knowledge.

> Truth is the end of the search. False or apparently true knowledge often intrudes itself upon the attention and at times it is so well disguised as to be dangerously deceptive. Man must learn of the universe, precisely as it is, or he cannot successfully find his place in it. A man should therefore use his reasoning faculty in all matters involving truth, and especially as concerning his religion.[3]

Truth is the end of our search. And what is truth? Knowledge of things as they really are, were, and will be. This knowledge, as discussed in Chapter 3, is present before God at all times. He literally sees truth. He sees the universe "precisely as it is." Unfortunately, we mortals are not so endowed. Our perception of the universe is limited not only by our obvious spatial constraints, but also by the fact that time for us is one-dimensional. What this means, in the context of this discussion, is that our acquiring of truth is a painfully slow and dangerously inaccurate process.

Our learning in mortality is, for the most part, sequential. We gather impressions, one after another, like pieces of an infinitely large jigsaw puzzle, hold them in our hands and heads, stare in bewilderment at them, try to fit them together, sometimes make mistakes, sometimes lose pieces we once possessed—and this is how we make sense of the universe which is our home. We do not see the whole picture, as God does. We learn "line upon line, precept on precept, here a little and there a little" (2 Nephi 28:30). God is gracious enough to have given us the gospel, the central pieces of the puzzle. Everything we then acquire through study or prayer we must try to attach to that central cluster of truths.

We speak of expanding the mortal mind, because that is how our learning takes place in mortality. We do not possess a sweeping, all-encompassing view of eternity; we do not see the end from the beginning or the beginning from the end. Rather, as we move down the mortal time line, we absorb seemingly random impressions of our corner of the universe. And we build our knowledge, adding one impression upon another. The longer we live, and the more diligent and observant we are, the more connections we make between things we have seen or heard or experienced. Patterns begin to emerge, pieces of the puzzle fall into place, and our mortal existence—at both the individual and collective level—begins to come into focus. We begin to understand our purpose here on earth, we recognize those activities and fields of knowledge that will help us develop our potential, and we identify pursuits and information that only waste our time.

To guide us and tutor us and help us make sense of our mortal experiences, God has given us divine assistance. First, we have the light of Christ, which serves to point us in the right direction and warn us when we stray. We also can qualify for the companionship of the Holy Ghost, who can tutor us and enlighten us, expanding our capacity to receive truth far beyond our natural mortal ability. Sometimes he merely whispers truth to our souls, sometimes he gives us brief flashes of intelligence, but now and then the Holy Spirit will give mortals a view of what learning is like in the eternities.

> And it came to pass . . . that Moses lifted up his eyes unto heaven, being filled with the Holy Ghost, which beareth record of the Father and the Son . . . . [And] Moses cast his eyes and

beheld the earth, yea, even all of it; and there was not a particle of it which he did not behold, discerning it by the spirit of God. And he beheld also the inhabitants thereof, and there was not a soul which he beheld not; and he discerned them by the Spirit of God; and their numbers were great, even numberless as the sand upon the sea shore" (Moses 1:24, 27-28).

Because of scriptural tidbits such as this one, I do not believe we will be sitting in school classrooms in the eternities, memorizing facts and taking multiple-choice tests. Rather, I imagine that the constraints that have been placed on our minds in mortality—for the sake of our being tested—will be removed then. We will no longer see "through a glass darkly," but will "know as also [we are] known" (1 Cor. 13:12).

If this is the case and learning in the eternities is so much more efficient, one might ask, "Why waste our time here on earth learning the hard way? Why not just focus on being obedient, repenting of our sins, and saving our souls?" Well, perhaps saving our souls is dependent, in part, on our attitude toward learning. As Joseph Smith suggested, knowledge is power, and the more knowledge we possess, the more power we have over Satan and his highly knowledgeable hoards. In other words, the more we know, the less easily we can be either deceived or tempted.

Behavior and Beliefs

Our behavior is a product of our beliefs. And incorrect beliefs, even when held at the subconscious level, can cause destructive behavior. If I believe, for instance, that men are better than women, I will inevitably behave in certain ways. I will likely be a domineering husband, making every decision, not listening to my wife's counsel, not allowing her to fully develop her talents and abilities, expecting her to be merely a decoration to give added luster to my bright and shining successes, or, worse, to live forever in my shadow.

If I believe that competitive, cut-throat capitalism is the true and only Christian economic system and that the business world is a morally neutral environment, I will behave in certain ways. I will charge as much as possible for goods and services I offer to others, pay as little as is acceptable to my employees, and take full advantage of every opportunity to increase my personal wealth—even if it comes at the expense of someone else or the environment. And I will not be prepared for the Lord's economic system, should he see fit to implement it once more.

If I believe that I can get closer to God in the mountains than in a noisy sacrament meeting, I will not find myself at Church as often as the Lord would like. Behavior follows belief, and some beliefs are admittedly subconscious. I may not even be aware of a false belief that moves me to action.

This is a good reason for learning of all kinds. As I grow in knowledge, I confirm some of my beliefs as true, others I see to be false. Regardless, increased knowledge helps me become conscious of things I assume are true and helps me correct inaccurate beliefs. The problem with not growing in knowledge is that we continue to follow many false principles, and our behavior may either injure others or damage our own spirits. The more complete our view of this mortal environment is, the better we understand the needs and motives and behaviors of others, the better equipped we are to act independently to do much good, and the less we will find ourselves acting on prejudice and ignorance.

As a new missionary on my way to Germany, my group of fourteen had a brief layover in Chicago. In the airport we were "accosted" by a couple of Hare Krishnas. They tried to sell us one of their books. When we turned them down, they offered to give it to us. I laughed and told them I'd just throw it in a garbage can before boarding the plane. One of them then looked me in the eye and said, "Maybe when you come back in two years, you'll be more open-minded." I laughed again. Open-mindedness was not something I believed in. I believed that "most open minds should be closed for repairs." Besides, I had THE TRUTH, and they didn't. Consequently, they didn't have anything of value to me. Their book was trash.

When I got to my initial assignment in the mission field, I related this experience to my first companion, thinking he would find it as amusing as I did. His response caught me off guard. He just shrugged and said, "You will be." Getting doors slammed in your face for two years, he knew, has a tendency to change your perspective about open-mindedness. I learned something during those two years about closed minds, and at the end of my mission, had I met the two Hare Krishnas in the airport, I definitely would have treated them differently.

Two Kinds of Learning

There are two basic types of learning in mortality: conceptual and experiential. In other words, we learn from experience, and we learn by acquiring mental concepts. And both aspects of knowledge are essential for our progress. With this in mind, I'd like to discuss five principles I have found to be true regarding conceptual and experiential knowledge.

1. *Conceptual knowledge without experience is barren.* It is possible for a blind person to become an expert in the theory of color and dimensions, to understand more than a sighted person about the

mechanics of seeing—how the nerves and tissues function to transmit visual images to the brain. But there are some things about seeing that one who is blind does not understand in the same way that those who experience sight understand them.

It is likewise possible for a person to learn Russian grammar and vocabulary, even acquire through much training and effort a Russian accent. But that person cannot really understand Russian until she has spent much time actually speaking with and listening to native Russians. Only in this way can she learn how the Russian mentality and culture are expressed through idiomatic phrases and various tones of speech.

Similarly, I might have an intellectual understanding of the gospel—even a fairly sound comprehension of doctrinal principles—and yet not really know the gospel. In religion, even more than in secular subjects, experience is crucial. Faith, for example, is but an idea until I have learned how to exercise it. Then faith becomes a principle of power. I can learn of repentance, recite its individual steps, but only when I partake of the atoning sacrifice and feel my sins forgiven do I truly understand what repentance is. I can recognize the necessity of forgiving others, but until I feel compassion in my soul, brush aside any animosity over harm that has come to me, and extend a Christlike love to someone who has wronged me, I know little about forgiveness.

Experience binds substance to the framework of conceptual knowledge. Experience and conceptual understanding are, to use a "literal" metaphor, like body and spirit, for it is the body that makes possible the experiences we could not have as spirits. As spirits we could only understand certain things in a sterile, conceptual manner.

2. *Conceptual knowledge opens the door to experience.* If the human race had never understood the basic principles of aerodynamics,

we would be incapable of experiencing the wonders of flight. Conceptual knowledge often precedes experience, makes experience possible.

If we do not possess the concept that God can hear and answer prayers, we will have no incentive to seek answers in prayer. If we do not understand that baptism can cleanse us of sin, we will see no need for baptism, and even if we were to be baptized, the ordinance would be largely ineffectual. If we do not understand the higher laws, we cannot keep them.

New knowledge will always open the door to new experience, because it sheds light on what is possible, but we must walk through that door or all the conceptual knowledge in the world will not save us. An expanding conceptual knowledge, if we permit it, can produce an expansion of experience, which enlarges the mortal mind and make us more like our Father in Heaven.

3. *Experience without conceptual knowledge does not help us progress.* Adam, when he was cast out of the Garden of Eden, offered sacrifice. He participated in the experience, but it was virtually meaningless to him because he didn't understand why he was doing it. When the angel came to him and explained the connection between animal sacrifice and the Savior's atonement, Adam's understanding was complete, and his experience took on new dimensions. With that conceptual key in hand, he could unlock the door of meaning and purpose behind his actions and find great power in them.

By the same token, if we partake of the sacrament without understanding its meaning, it lacks power in our lives—the experience becomes hollow. But if we comprehend the symbolic significance of the bread and water and partake of them knowing what they represent, we can renew our covenants and receive a weekly remission of our sins.

4. *Conceptual knowledge adds stability to experiential knowledge.* When I received my witness of the truthfulness of the gospel, it came not as a warm feeling of confirmation, but as an unexpected and electrifying encounter with the Spirit. I "felt" with complete certainty in every fiber of my being that the gospel, as restored through Joseph Smith, was true. I had been told so in an unmistakable way. But I was young, and my mind had not yet expanded sufficiently to comprehend exactly what I had experienced. I remember distinctly how insecure I felt in my new knowledge. I couldn't deny the experience, but when someone would bring up a doubt or seeming contradiction about the Church that I had no explanation for, I would find myself, as Joseph Smith would put it, flying to pieces like glass, wondering exactly what was and wasn't true.

It was not until I had spent much time studying and pondering the gospel, fitting the pieces together into a cohesive whole in my own mind, that I gained true stability and firmness in my testimony. Once I grasped intellectually, at least in a small way, the beauty and perfection of the gospel, that initial experience (the witness of the Spirit) became an immovable anchor in my soul. The two types of knowledge complemented each other. Separately, they were inadequate.

5. *Sin and guilt prevent the mind from expanding.* If we do not keep the commandments, we will be unable to gain those experiences that matter in the eternal sense, and we will not be in a condition to receive light and truth, conceptual understanding. Especially when the mind is burdened by guilt, it cannot expand. Guilt is a constricting, distracting force that leaves no peace for any significant type of learning. In other words, before the mind can expand to encompass more light and truth, the soul must be striving to keep the commandments and become like God.

The Constricted Mind

The constricted mind, as opposed to the expanding mind, believes that it already possesses THE TRUTH and shouldn't be nosing around for more knowledge than God has seen fit to give. "Everything that we need has been revealed," I've heard some people say. "We just need to start living the principles that have been revealed." Of course we do, but living established principles sometimes becomes much easier when we are adding to them, when we feel that we are making actual progress in the accumulation of knowledge. An excitement about expanding our intelligence can motivate us to live according to the knowledge we already have. To put it bluntly, the problem is not that we have too much knowledge in the Church. The scriptures suggest that the most important thing we can do is to prepare ourselves to receive much, much more than has been given.

Hugh Nibley chides us, not so gently, about the difference between what we too often settle for and what we should be striving for. He claims we give

> young people and old awards for zeal alone, zeal without knowledge—for sitting in endless meetings, for dedicated conformity, and unlimited capacity for suffering boredom. We think it more commendable to get up at 5:00 a.m. to write a bad book than to get up at nine o'clock to write a good one—that is pure zeal that tends to breed a race of insufferable, self-righteous prigs and barren minds. One only has to consider the present outpouring of "inspirational" books in the Church which bring little new in the way of knowledge: truisms, and platitudes, kitsch, and clichés have become our everyday diet. The Prophet would never settle for that. "I advise you to go on to perfection and

search deeper and deeper into the mysteries of Godliness. . . . It has always been my province to dig up hidden mysteries, new things, for my hearers."[4]

Without new knowledge we stagnate—both intellectually and experientially. Without discussion of significant new ideas we do not improve ourselves. If this book is trying to say anything, it is that we as individual Latter-day Saints do not see life from the same vantage point and, hence, do not believe exactly the same things. A surprisingly wide diversity of gospel interpretations can be found among members of the Church. And there is good reason for this. We simply don't know with any certainty many things about mortality, eternity, and the gospel, because the Lord has not yet revealed anything about them. And sometimes his revelations can be understood to mean many different things. This leaves us to believe what we will, and those beliefs are colored by our own personal experiences and perspectives. Because of this fact, it is critical that we seek new knowledge, not only through revelation, but also through vigorous debate, in which we examine the things we do not yet understand or about which we disagree.

Contrary to popular opinion, speculation is not all bad, if we take it for what it is and for what it can offer us. Alma speculated about the resurrection for his son's benefit (cf. Alma: 40:20), then recorded his "opinion" in scripture. Speculation and reasoning and discussion can induce us to ponder and pray for greater enlightenment. They can help us see things in a new, perhaps a more complete, light. The truth need not shy away from any amount of scrutiny. It is only error that fears illumination. Error constricts the mind, reduces its uniqueness. Truth expands it, as does the honest search for truth.

11

Seeing and Seeking Miracles

On the sunny morning of July 7, 1977, I packed my bags, lugged them a kilometer to the subway station, rode the U-bahn with my companion to Tegel Flughafen in West Berlin, and boarded a Pan Am 737 with Elder Meacham and Sister Thorpe. Together we flew to Hamburg, where the mission's dark green Volkswagen bus picked us up and whisked us off to the mission office to join the other twelve missionaries who were also going home the next morning. It was a strange and disorienting day, and perhaps I can blame my jumbled memory of it on the fact that my mind was still in Berlin, while my body was in Hamburg. All I remember is a whirlwind of activity, aimed at getting us reoriented toward going home and somehow fitting in again in what had become to us a foreign land. But out of that whirlwind, one thin slice of memory remains surprisingly clear.

At some point during that afternoon or evening, the fifteen of us had a testimony meeting with the mission president and his staff. I don't remember what I said when my turn came; I don't remember what any of the elders said; but I remember vividly the testimony Sister Thorpe shared with us. She explained that in the interview with her stake president, eighteen months earlier, she had divulged a secret desire of her heart. "I want to see miracles on my mission," she had confided to him. Then, almost apologetically, she had asked him if it was wrong to seek miracles. He had assured her it was not wrong. She related this conversation to us, and then, after a brief pause, testified: "I've seen miracles on my mission."

I'd never considered my own experiences of the previous two years in that context, but that day I had to confess that I, too, had seen miracles on my mission. And over the years I've come to understand something. I saw more miracles on my mission than I ever realized while they were happening. In a way, I guess, I was blind to them. Unlike Sister Thorpe, I wasn't looking for miracles. And I think I missed out on some important feelings and knowledge and experiences because of that.

Elder LeGrand Richards used to like to quote a poem by Elizabeth Barrett Browning that explains my blindness:

Earth's crammed with heaven,
And every common bush afire with God;
But only he who sees takes off his shoes;
The rest sit round it and pluck blackberries.[1]

Most of the time I'm very busy plucking blackberries. But every now and then I step back and look around me, and I see the hand of God in places I had never suspected. "And in nothing doth man offend God," he tells us, "or against none is his wrath kindled, save those who confess not his hand in all things, and obey not his commandments" (D&C 59:21). I understand that condemnation, and I think I know why God feels so strongly about our looking for his hand in our own lives and in the lives of others. It's not because he wants the recognition. It's because he is trying to teach us something through his intervention in our mortal existence. Miracles are hints and clues about who we are and who we can become.

"God Specializes in the Impossible"

What is a miracle? A good definition, I suppose, is that a miracle is something God can do which we can't. It is usually some act that lies beyond both our power to perform and our ability to understand. But a miracle is not a miracle to God. Miracles, to him, are as ordinary as, say, driving a car is to us. Once, talking about faith in Christ, a great teacher made this statement: "God specializes in the impossible." If we could do everything for ourselves, we would not need God. But we can't do everything for ourselves. We need his assistance. Indeed, sometimes we need the impossible. And he is there.

Miracles are one way in which God serves us. He is doing things for us that we can't do for ourselves. That is, I believe, the purest form of service. As always, he is showing us an example. He wants us to do likewise. And perhaps the best laboratory for us to experiment with this aspect of our divine potential is parenthood. The parallels between parenthood and Godhood are numerous, for God is, of course, the perfect parent.

To children, many of the things parents can do are miracles. Mothers and fathers can do things that are impossible in their children's eyes. As children grow, however, their view of the impossible changes. For a baby, holding a bottle or changing a diaper are impossible and much appreciated acts that might well be considered miracles. For a toddler, reaching a high cupboard and driving a car are impossible. For young children, making a living is nothing short of miraculous. I have a first-grader, and to him money just magically appears. (From my point of view, it magically disappears!) The sarcastic parental question, "Do you think money grows on trees?" is actually a perfectly valid question. To a five-year-old, money growing on trees makes just as much sense as our system of employment and banking. God, I imagine, could ask us similar questions: "Do you think forgiveness grows on trees?" "Do you think the cure for blindness grows on trees?" "Do you think revelation grows on trees?" Sometimes it may seem to us that such blessings are conjured up with some sort of magic, because they are beyond our comprehension. But to God, these acts of service and love are simple and ordinary matters, for he operates and understands at a different level than we do.

Our children, as discussed above, view the things we do with more than a touch of admiration and envy—up to a certain age. For teenagers, of course, there are no miracles. Parents cannot seem to do anything right, much less miraculous. And there is a parallel here, too. Do we sometimes get stuck in a teenage relationship with our Eternal Father? Do we become so independent and distant and unbelieving and presumably self-sufficient that we don't ask God for miracles, don't permit him to serve us, don't recognize his hand behind the scenes? When we earn our mortal drivers licenses, do we use them to run as far from our Eternal Father as we can, not even realizing it's his car we took and that he bought the gas?

Dispensing miracles as a parent is a balancing act, and we can learn much from our Father in Heaven. We don't want to do more for our children than is good for their development—I'm reminded of a boy scout I once knew who couldn't even open a cereal box by himself—but neither do we want to turn a deaf ear to their requests and cries for help.

Sometimes when my children demand that I do things for them that they can do for themselves, I find myself sarcastically responding, "Am I your slave?" The unspoken message here is two-fold: first, "Ask politely," and second, "Do it yourself—you're big enough." Sometimes I'm not sure whether I say this out of exhaustion, laziness, or concern for their growth, but I am *not* their slave, and they should not treat me as such. I am, however, their servant, in the same respect that God is our servant. He serves us not only because he loves us, but because he wants to teach us how to serve. He doesn't want us to order him around and demand things of him, and he sometimes refuses to do things for us when we can do them for ourselves, but he is never sarcastic with us. He is encouraging even when silent, and wants us to learn to be independent as he is.

I should learn from this, and instead of responding with "Am I your slave?" I should probably say something like, "I'd love to do it for you, but I think you can do it yourself." Children tend to complain when you say things like this, but if they really want what they have asked you to do, and if they are big enough to do it themselves, they will eventually get around to it, and will grow in the process.

If we can learn to view ourselves as eternal beings who are here in the school of mortality learning how to become like our Eternal Parents, we will be better servants—of our children and of others. We will recognize that as we increase in knowledge, we increase in our ability and power to serve, to do things for others that they cannot do for themselves. We will also more accurately discern when others are capable and should be allowed to do for themselves.

Knowledge and Wonder

Becoming like our Heavenly Parents implies that we will gradually lose the sense of wide-eyed wonder with which we regard their works—much as our children lose their sense of wonder about the things we adults do. As they begin to understand the mechanics of driving a car, or as they grow tall enough to climb on countertops and reach the cupboards themselves, they cease viewing these acts as extraordinary. So it is with miracles. As we grow and understand more completely how God works, though we still view him with awe, it is an awe that is bound to knowledge rather than ignorance. Let me illustrate.

We have all seen, at least on TV, space shuttles boosted into the heavens by enormous rockets. Many of us remember clearly the first moon landing. I was a deacon at the time, and I can still remember how we gathered at our advisor's house and sat glued to the black-and-white tube, watching this utterly amazing feat. I am still in awe of this fact, that men and women can travel into space, even to the moon, and return safely. But my amazement has changed over the years. As a thirteen-year-old, the moon landing was beyond comprehension, almost beyond belief, more like a science-fiction movie than reality. Over the years, however, I have come to understand some of the physics, as well as some of the manufacturing technology, that needed to be developed for these flights into space. I understand, for instance, that many obstacles had to be overcome—everything from creating and packaging foods that can easily be eaten in a weightless environment to inventing and producing materials that can withstand the intense heat of reentering the earth's atmosphere. I understand also that the margins for error are infinitesimal. If a machine has 1,000 parts, for example, and each part has a 99.9 percent chance of working correctly, there is still only a 36.77 percent ($.999^{1000}$) chance that the machine as a whole will function properly. A space shuttle has many more than 1,000 parts. Given this fact, I find it utterly astounding that we have not had more disasters. My awe now is more a sense of admiration for the intelligence and accuracy of those involved in these undertakings. I was especially impressed when I learned that the huge computers used to guide the first moon landing had less capacity than computers we can now carry in one hand like a notebook.

The computer is, of course, another miraculous invention that seems almost magical to the beginner. This entire book, for instance, takes up only about .05 percent of the space on my computer's hard drive. I have software installed on this machine that can create marvelous graphics and lay out pages ready for printing. These are effects, however, and to the mere user or observer, they are incredible. But a person who knows something about the theory from which computers sprang or the manufacturing of microscopic circuits or the collective brilliance required to create the software that makes the computer such a marvelous invention—that person has a different kind of appreciation, an appreciation based on knowledge. Fittingly, those who know the most also see possibilities for new and expanded applications.

I am not suggesting when we grow and gain intelligence that we bring God, in our minds, down to our level; rather, that we raise ourselves up and come nearer his level. We still stand in awe of his love and intelligence and power and perfection, but we see him as an example of what we can become, rather than as being so far beyond us that we cannot even hope to comprehend him. As we expand our mortal minds in this manner, we are no longer surprised by God's miracles, but look for them, even actively seek them. God's prophets from the beginning have had a distinctive attitude toward miracles. They weren't surprised by them, and they didn't just hope for them. They expected miracles. The Brother of Jared fully expected the Lord to make his sixteen stones shine with light. Peter at the temple gates did not just hope God would cure the lame man; he commanded him to rise, reached out his hand, and lifted him up. Moses didn't worry that the Red Sea perhaps wouldn't part. He stretched out his hand, fully expecting the waters to divide asunder. What we're talking about here is faith. That is how miracles usually come. When we partake of the sacrament, if we simply wish we could be cleansed of sin, the miracle of forgiveness will likely not occur. We must partake, expecting to be cleansed of our sins.

Natural Laws?

We generally assume that God performs miracles by obeying natural laws that we are not aware of. Jesus turned water into wine not with magic but with his knowledge of some higher principle that we still do not comprehend. Perhaps this is so, perhaps not. We really don't know how God operates in performing miracles. Orson Pratt, in a *Millennial Star* article titled "The Holy Spirit," offers an interesting explanation of how God works on and through the elements.

> From what the revealed word has stated upon this subject, we can confidently assert, that the Holy Spirit exists, not only as a personage, but also as an inexhaustible quantity of substance, pervading all worlds, like heat or electricity, being diffused through and round about all masses of other matter, governing and controlling all things, according to the mind of the Father and the Son. That part of this substance which exists

as a person, cannot be in more than one place at the same instant. . . . [B]ut the Holy Spirit existing not only as a person, but in infinite quantities, can by parts of its essence, extend through the universe. No one part of this essence can be in two places at the same time. It requires an infinite quantity in order to occupy infinite space.[2]

This discussion is continued in the next issue, offering an even more surprising description of how God dwells in all substances, producing the "variety of forces" and "motions" that are "generally ascribed to nature."

All of the great laws of the universe are not the laws of inert matter, but the laws of a self-moving, intelligent, and powerful matter, possessing knowledge, goodness, love, and every other attribute that is good, and great, and useful. . . . The force that causes the particles of a piece of iron to adhere to each other, is the same force that causes the iron to sink in water; and the force that causes iron to sink in water, is the same force that caused the axe to swim by the command of Elisha; it is an intelligent, self-moving force, and, therefore, can vary its usual mode of operation when it pleases. The swimming of iron is no more a miracle than the sinking of iron, they are both the effects of the same cause . . . .

When God performs a miracle by suspending a law of nature, he does so, not by acting at a distance . . . , but by the actual presence of those parts of his essence which are in contact with the materials on which the miracle is performed.[3]

These are interesting ideas about how God works, suggesting it is not necessarily some immutable natural law that God follows, but rather the exertion of his divine will, which pervades and surrounds all matter. It is good, I believe, for us to consider such ideas, because they may broaden our perspective about how we, when we have reached our eternal potential, will live and operate in blessing the lives of our spirit offspring. And that is the focus of everything we learn in mortality. We are learning to be gods, to be like our Eternal Parents. Their work and glory is centered in us, just as our work and glory—the focus of our existence—will be directed toward our children.

Individual Miracles

God's miracles are, for the most part, individual in nature. At times he will feed five thousand, but most often he reaches out and touches the blind Bartimæuses of the world. And most of his miracles are not flashy, attention-grabbing displays of divine intervention. Usually he works quietly, behind the scenes, and expects us to open our spiritual eyes and see—and take off our shoes.

In my own family, the only glaringly visible miracle we have been blessed with was Troy's survival. After being born three months early, with lungs that were severely underdeveloped (from being in utero without amniotic fluid for a whole month), Troy's chances, according to medical science were slim. That first night, after the neonatologist had worked on him for several hours with no success, he turned to me and prepared me for what he saw as the inevitable conclusion to the little drama taking place in the newborn ICU. He said it didn't look good. Nothing they had tried was working. In essence, Troy wouldn't make it. But weeks before, I had prayed earnestly about this child, wanting to give an appropriate priesthood blessing, and God had granted me a tiny miracle—a whisper of revelation, assuring me a greater miracle was in store and this child would survive. I took in the doctor's words silently, calmly. How do you tell a medical expert that he's wrong, that he doesn't have all the facts? I just watched patiently and with considerable interest as the doctor's "last resort" miraculously worked. Somehow oxygen passed from the tiny, damaged lungs into the bloodstream. And the fight began. For weeks doctors and nurses cautioned us, even openly predicting that Troy would have severe handicaps. We watched and waited and struggled and sometimes wept with frustration because this miracle was unfolding so slowly and so painfully. But Troy proved the doctors and nurses wrong. As I write he is nearly seven, he is healthy, and he is a constant reminder to us that God does work miracles, that he does know and love each of his children, that he has an active hand in each of our lives.

Troy is somewhat unique in that he was the recipient of a very visible miracle. But his uniqueness ends with the word "visible." I have come to know that no life is without divine intervention. As a missionary, as a home teacher, as a parent, as a Gospel Doctrine teacher, as a member of a bishopric, as a Primary teacher, I have seen the hand of God touching the lives of individuals. I have even sought his intervention on behalf of others at times. I should do it more often, much more often, because it exercises my faith, makes it stronger, and blesses lives. We are commanded, in fact, to constantly seek divine intervention in our own lives, to seek miracles, as it were:

> Yea, cry unto him for mercy; for he is mighty to save.
> Yea, humble yourselves, and continue in prayer unto him.
> Cry unto him when ye are in your fields, yea, over all your
> flocks.

Cry unto him in your houses, yea, over all your household, both morning, mid-day, and evening.

Yea, cry unto him against the power of your enemies.

Yea, cry unto him against the devil, who is an enemy to all righteousness.

Cry unto him over the crops of your fields, that ye may prosper in them.

Cry over the flocks of your fields, that they may increase. (Alma 34:18-25.)

God wants to bless us, as individuals, as families, as wards, as a church. He wants to work miracles, do the impossible in our behalf. And he wants us to grow in our capacity to work our own tiny miracles in each other's lives.

Conclusion

You Can Take It With You

One of the great hazards of this mortal existence is the temptation to forget our primary purpose here, to spend too much of our time and energy on those things that have no eternal significance. This world is so full of distractions, many of them forced upon us by the socioeconomic and political systems in which we live, that we sometimes get deflected from the important matters of mortality. If I spend the days of my life busily jumping through Babylon's economic hoops, acquiring material possessions, watching television, pursuing the applause of others, and seeking worldly entertainment, I may someday be shocked to find that "the harvest is past, the summer is ended, and my soul is not saved!" (D&C 56:16.)

Some acquisitions in this life are more critical than others. Some have eternal value. Others have only a secondary or auxiliary value—they help us obtain the eternally significant possessions. Material acquisitions of all sorts have of course a secondary value. They are, to paraphrase an early prophet of this dispensation, like a hill of dung—only useful for bringing forth more fruit. "You can't take it with you," we're told. And that is true for material acquisitions and worldly fame. Thus, if our primary focus in this life is the acquiring of money and celebrity, we will enter the immortal realms in a state of spiritual poverty and obscurity. But some possessions, some of the gains we've made in this life, we *can* take with us. Indeed, when we begin to consider which mortal acquisitions and attributes we can carry with us through the veil, we also begin to define the pursuits we should be focusing on in this life. What can we take with us? The following list is not exhaustive, but it does suggest a few items.

Knowledge

"Whatever principle of intelligence we attain unto in this life, it will rise with us in the resurrection. And if a person gains more knowledge and intelligence in this life through diligence and obedience than another, he will have so much the advantage in the world to come" (D&C 130:18-19). As discussed in detail in Chapter 9, we should diligently seek knowledge all the days of our lives. "Seek ye out of the best books words of wisdom; seek learning, even by study and also by faith" (D&C 88:118).

For nine years I taught business management at BYU, and I used to ask my students—the majority of whom were returned missionaries, juniors and seniors at the university—if they had read certain books considered classics of thought and literature. Their response was consistently depressing to me—apparently only a handful took their university education seriously. The rest spent all their intellectual effort on marketing and finance texts, *The Wall Street Journal*, and *Fortune*. When I asked them about their extracurricular reading, they looked at me like I had a screw loose. "You're not suggesting we read books just for the sake of learning something new and expanding our mental horizons?" their eyes would say. "You've got to be kidding. We can succeed in life without reading all that impractical stuff." Most of my students, I know, were at the university for one reason—to get a good job. And they looked forward to graduation so that they could get on with the more important matters of life.

But the important matters of life happen to include obtaining knowledge—of all kinds. Quoting the Prophet Joseph, Hugh Nibley writes, "'We consider that God has created man with a mind capable of instruction, and a faculty which may be enlarged in proportion to the heed and diligence given to the light communicated from heaven to the intellect . . . but . . . no man ever arrived in a moment: he must have been instructed by proper degrees.' . . . Note well that the Prophet makes no distinction between things of the spirit and things of the intellect."[1]

Is it possible that we have created a mental Maginot Line between intellectualism and spirituality that is as useless as the geographical one proved to be? I would suggest that these two aspects of our identity are merely two parts of the same wonderful whole that should overlap completely. To be unintellectually spiritual is probably at least as damnable as being unspiritually intellectual. It suggests a disdain for knowledge, which is perhaps the main ingredient in discovering who we really are and in developing the eternally unique personality each of us possesses now in rudimentary form. The more true knowledge we gain, the better able we are to define ourselves, recognize our potential, discern Satan's ploys, serve others, and find our proper place in the eternal scheme of things.

Suffice it to say that any true knowledge—whether produced

by intellectual reasoning, scientific experimentation, divine revelation, or personal experience—will rise with us in the resurrection. We can take it with us. It is a currency that is at least as negotiable beyond the veil as it is here. And perhaps the most important aspect of knowledge we can acquire in this life is the ability to think. The ability to think for ourselves, to be independently and creatively righteous, is a Godlike attribute that helps define and enhance our uniqueness and individuality.

Talents

The innate and acquired abilities we develop here will not be lost when we die. Mozart's incredible musical genius, Einstein's theoretical brilliance, Goethe's breathtaking command of language, Monet's artistic sensitivity—these talents did not vanish at death. Not all talents, however, are equal in eternal reckoning. One's facility at financial accounting, I suppose, will be in short demand in the eternities, as will be a dentist's skill at filling teeth. These are temporary talents that should not be exalted above the permanent ones we are commanded to develop.

Certain talents come as specifically named gifts of the Spirit. Wisdom, knowledge, faith, prophecy, miracles, tongues, charity— all these spiritual gifts have value in the eternal realms. And we are commanded to seek them.

Bodies

This may be a surprising thought, but it shouldn't be. Yes, we can take our bodies with us—after a brief separation. And though the resurrected body will be renewed and made immortal, how we treat the body in this life may partially determine the state of the body after the resurrection. Spencer W. Kimball said:

> When we take precautions to protect ourselves from hazards, accidents, death, we are thinking not only of saving ourselves from suffering, from pain, from expense, but [of preserving] our bodies for their eternal destiny. . . .
>
> Some sectarian peoples minimize the body and look forward to freedom from it. Some flail and beat and torture the body, but the gospel of Jesus Christ magnifies the importance of the body and the dignity of man. This body will come forth in the resurrection. It will be free from all imperfections and scars and infirmities which came to it in mortality which were not self-inflicted. Would we have a right to expect a perfect body if we carelessly or intentionally damaged it?
>
> We shall have our resurrected, perfected bodies through the eternities. They were given to us—we had little to do with getting them.
>
> It then becomes our duty to protect them from hazards, from mutilation or disfigurement. We should treat them well, building them with proper foods, proper rest, proper exercise and keep them strong, robust, beautiful, and undamaged and live on and on till called home by our Lord.[2]

As discussed in Chapter 2, those who do not use the body to pursue righteousness, who are consequently assigned to the lesser kingdoms after the resurrection, will have certain functions and aspects of the body deleted or altered. Only by correctly using our bodies to seek righteousness can we expect eventually to have those bodies perfected with the full capacities of godhood.

After the resurrection, as our intelligences, spirits, and bodies are welded into an exalted, inseparable whole, we will finally become complete individuals for eternity. For only when body and spirit are inseparably connected can we "receive a fulness of joy" (D&C 93:33).

Weaknesses

We do not leave this life perfect. We leave in various degrees of imperfection. This means that we will take certain weaknesses through the veil with us. Only Christ was sinless in this life. But we can continue our progress toward eternal perfection after this life, if our course during mortality was pointing toward that ultimate destination. It has been said that our spiritual condition at death is less important than the direction in which we are moving.

Only God who knows all can judge us, but it is important for us to isolate and, through Christ's grace, overcome as many weaknesses in this life as possible. From what we have been told, spiritual weaknesses will be harder to conquer when we have no bodies. And it seems reasonable that before God will entrust us with a perfect body, our spirits must also achieve a degree of perfection worthy of such a great gift.

Memories

Part of the knowledge we will take with us consists of our memories. These memories, as discussed in Chapter 3, are incomplete and two-dimensional. We will have restored to us, however, a more perfect memory. Jacob tells us that after the resurrection we shall have "a perfect knowledge like unto us in the flesh, save it be that our knowledge shall be perfect. Wherefore, we shall have a perfect knowledge of all our guilt, and our uncleanness, and our nakedness; and the righteous shall have a perfect knowledge of their enjoyment, and their righteousness" (2 Nephi 9:13-14).

I have often longed for a more perfect memory of certain experiences in my life. The moment when I first met my wife is a memory I wish I could preserve perfectly. The cauldron of feelings I experienced as I returned home from the mission field, the wonder of feeling the Spirit for the first time, the joy of holding our first baby, the incredible beauty of one perfect evening in Rothenburg, Germany—these memories and many more I wish I had full access to. But, as it is with us in mortality, these memories are locked away somewhere inside where I cannot reach them in complete form. Even the feelings those memories once evoked have faded.

Wouldn't it be wonderful to have a perfect memory of our "enjoyments," a memory so complete that it would be like experiencing the enjoyment again? That, apparently, is what we are promised. But that gift, as Jacob reminds us, cuts both ways. We will also have a perfect memory of our sinful, painful experiences. This should be a great incentive for us not only to live righteously and repent of our mistakes, but to live life fully—with passion, sensitivity, and an eye to the beauty around us.

Passions

We will take our passions with us when we depart this life. Some of them may still be unrefined, may be governed by weaknesses, but God is a God of body, parts, and passions. He has perfected, refined passions. As we reach for our eternal potential, our passions will also become refined, like the Father's. These Godlike forces of internal opposition through which we respond to mortal experience help define our uniqueness, express our individuality, and create a perfect, eternal identity.

Relationships

The feelings we have for each other will survive death. The bonds that hold us together as family, friends, and brothers and sisters in Christ will be among our most priceless possessions in the eternal worlds. There those relationships will blossom and bear new fruit, for we will be able to communicate and understand one another in a more perfect manner. We will be able to share feelings and experiences in a way mortality does not permit. There our memories of eternity-long associations will be restored and added to the memories of our mortal associations.

These relationships, this diversity of other personalities we come in contact with, will continue to paint for us a varied backdrop against which we can see more clearly our own uniqueness. What this means for us now, is that we should work to develop meaningful, genuine relationships in which we allow others the freedom to express their individuality and in which we allow our own undistorted personalities to shine brightly.

Identity

All these other elements of self that survive the journey through the veil combine to give us a sense of identity, a unique personality, or, if you will, individuality. That identity will be with us for eternity. It is our destiny, and we are moving toward it one step at a time. This should be our most important pursuit in mortality—this development of an eternally perfect identity. Our greatest help in this sacred endeavor is the Holy Ghost, who knows us intimately. In Parley P. Pratt's eloquent description of how the Holy Spirit influences us, note the emphasis on these traits and acquisitions that we will be able to take with us through the veil:

The gift of the Holy Spirit adapts itself to all these organs or attributes. It quickens all the intellectual faculties, increases, enlarges, expands and purifies all the natural passions and affections; and adapts them, by the gift of wisdom, to their lawful use. It inspires, develops, cultivates and matures all the fine-toned sympathies, joys, tastes, kindred feelings and affections of our nature. It inspires virtue, kindness, goodness, tenderness, gentleness and charity. It develops beauty of person, form and features. It tends to health, vigor, animation and social feeling. It develops and invigorates all the faculties of the physical and intellectual man. It strengthens, invigorates, and gives tone to the nerves. In short, it is, as it were, marrow to the bone, joy to the heart, light to the eyes, music to the ears, and life to the whole being.

In the presence of such persons, one feels to enjoy the light of their countenances, as the genial rays of a sunbeam. Their very atmosphere diffuses a thrill, a warm glow of pure gladness and sympathy, to the heart and nerves of others who have kindred feelings, or sympathy of spirit.[3]

Mortality is the great testing period. Earth life is not intended to be easy. It is not easy to walk by faith while the world around us is chasing the artificial and worldly identities Satan would have us acquire. Only by keeping first things first and recognizing auxiliary pursuits for what they are can we stay on the path that leads to godhood. We are children of God, individuals with immense potential and infinite worth. For this reason it is of supreme importance that we discover in this life who we are and who we can become, and that we also discover the great Mediator who stands ready to help us achieve our glorious potential.

Notes

Introduction

[1] Joseph Fielding Smith, comp., *Teachings of the Prophet Joseph Smith* (Salt Lake City: Deseret Book Co., 1942), p. 331; hereafter cited as *Teachings*.

[2] Joseph Smith, *History of The Church of Jesus Christ of Latter-day Saints*, ed. B.H. Roberts, 7 vols. (Salt Lake City: The Church of Jesus Christ of Latter-day Saints, 1932-51), 3:295-96; hereafter cited as *HC*.

[3] Brigham Young in *Journal of Discourses*, 26 vols. (London: Latter-day Saints' Book Depot, 1855-86), 13:153, hereafter cited as *JD*.

[4] *JD* 8:185.

Chapter 1

[1] *Teachings*, pp. 353-54.

[2] *Teachings*, p. 354.

[3] *Teachings*, p. 354.

Chapter 2
[1] Joseph Fielding Smith, *Doctrines of Salvation* (Salt Lake City: Bookcraft, Inc., 1955), vol. 2. p. 288.
[2] George G. Ritchie, with Elizabeth Sherrill, *Return from Tomorrow* (Old Tappan, New Jersey: Spire Books, 1978), p. 69, italics mine.

Chapter 3
[1] *Lectures on Faith*, N.B. Lundwall, Compiler (Salt Lake City: Bookcraft, Inc.), Lecture Third, verses 2-5, p. 33.
[2] Neal A. Maxwell, *The Ensign*, "Speaking Today," February, 1979, p. 72.
[3] *Lectures on Faith*, p. 56.
[4] Hugh W. Nibley, "Zeal Without Knowledge" in *Nibley on the Timely and the Timeless* (Provo: Religious Studies Center, Brigham Young University, 1978), p. 264.
[5] *Lectures on Faith*, Lecture Seventh, verse 3, p. 61.
[6] *Return from Tomorrow*, pp. 49-50.
[7] *Return from Tomorrow*, pp. 48-49.

Chapter 4
[1] David O. McKay, *Gospel Ideals* (Salt Lake City: Deseret Book Co., 1953), pp. 347-48.
[2] Glen M. Roylance, "Putting Off the Natural Man," a taped speech delivered in the Germany Hamburg Mission, 1978.
[3] *Answers to Gospel Questions*, 3 Vols. (Salt Lake City: Deseret Book Co., 1966), vol. 3, p. 100.

Chapter 5
[1] As told by Glen M. Roylance in "Putting Off the Natural Man."

Chapter 6
[1] Bible Dictionary in LDS editions of the Bible, p. 697.
[2] *Teachings*, pp. 346-47.
[3] *Teachings*, p. 150.

Chapter 7
[1] Hugh W. Nibley, "But What Kind of Work?" in *Approaching Zion*, pp. 270-71.

Chapter 8
[1] "'Mirror, Mirror on the Wall': A Look at the 'Me Decade,'" *1979 Devotional Speeches of the Year*, (Provo: Brigham Young University Press, 1980), p. 45.
[2] "The Business of Leisure," a special report in *The Wall Street Journal*, Monday, April 21, 1986, p. 2D.

Chapter 9
[1] Neil W. Chamberlain, *The Limits of Corporate Responsibility* (New York: Basic Books, 1973), p. 92.
[2] Lyndall Urwick, "Organization as a Technical Problem," in *Papers on the Science of Administration*, eds. Luther Gulick and Lyndall Urwick (New York: Institute of Public Administration, 1937), p. 85.
[3] David K. Hart, "The Sympathetic Organization," in *Papers on the Ethics of Administration*, ed. N. Dale Wright (Provo: Brigham Young University, 1988), pp. 76-77.
[4] *HC*, 3:295-96.

Chapter 10
[1] *Teachings*, p. 217.
[2] *Teachings*, p. 137.

[3] John A. Widtsoe, *A Rational Theology* (Salt Lake City: General Boards of the Mutual Improvement Associations, 1932), pp. 7-8.
[4] Hugh W. Nibley, "Zeal Without Knowledge," *Nibley on the Timely and the Timeless* (Provo: Religious Studies Center, Brigham Young University, 1978), pp. 270-71.

Chapter 11
[1] As quoted by LeGrand Richards in "'Earth's Crammed With Heaven': Reminiscences," *1977 Devotional Speeches of the Year*, (Provo: Brigham Young University, 1978), p. 159.
[2] "The Holy Spirit," *The Millennial Star*, Vol.. XII, No. 20, p. 308.
[3] "The Holy Spirit," *The Millennial Star*, Vol.. XII, No. 21, p. 327.

Conclusion
[1] Hugh W. Nibley, *Nibley on the Timely and the Timeless* (Provo: Religious Studies Center at BYU, 1978), p. 268.
[2] *The Teachings of Spencer W. Kimball*, ed. Edward L. Kimball (Salt Lake City: Bookcraft, 1982), pp. 36-37.
[3] Parley P. Pratt, *Key to the Science of Theology*, 10th ed. (Salt Lake City: Deseret Book Co., 1966), p. 101.

Index